JavaScript at Scale

Build enduring JavaScript applications with scaling
insights from the front-line of JavaScript development

Adam Boduch

[PACKT] open source*
PUBLISHING   community experience distilled
BIRMINGHAM - MUMBAI

JavaScript at Scale

First published: July 2015

Production reference: 1270715

Published by Packt Publishing Ltd.
Livery Place
35 Livery Street
Birmingham B3 2PB, UK.

ISBN 978-1-78528-215-7

www.packtpub.com

Credits

Author
Adam Boduch

Reviewers
August N. Marcello III
Yogesh Singh
Nikolay Sokolov
Serkan Yersen

Commissioning Editor
Edward Gordon

Acquisition Editors
Kevin Colaco
Owen Roberts

Content Development Editor
Divij Kotian

Technical Editor
Ryan Kochery

Copy Editor
Angad Singh

Project Coordinator
Nikhil Nair

Proofreader
Safis Editing

Indexer
Rekha Nair

Graphics
Jason Monteiro

Production Coordinator
Melwyn Dsa

Cover Work
Melwyn Dsa

About the Author

Adam Boduch has been involved with large-scale JavaScript development for nearly 10 years. Before moving to the frontend, he worked on several large-scale cloud computing products using Python and Linux. No stranger to complexity, Adam has practical experience with real-world software systems and the scaling challenges they pose. He is the author of several JavaScript books, including *Lo-Dash Essentials,* and is passionate about innovative user experiences and high performance.

Adam lives in Toronto and is a senior software engineer at Virtustream.

I'd like to thank my mom and dad.

About the Reviewers

August N. Marcello III is a highly passionate software engineer with nearly 2 decades of experience in the design, implementation, and deployment of modern client-side web application architectures in the enterprise. An exclusive focus on delivering compelling SaaS based user experiences throughout the web ecosystem has proven both personally and professionally rewarding for him. His passion for emerging technologies in general, combined with a particular focus on forward-thinking JavaScript platforms, has been a primary driver in his pursuit of technical excellence. When he's not coding, he can be found trail running, mountain biking, and spending time with family and friends. Visit him online at www.augustmarcello.com.

> Many thanks to Chuck, Mark, Eric, and Adam, with whom I had the privilege to work and learn. Gratitude to my family, friends, and the experiences I have been blessed to be a part of.

Yogesh Singh graduated in computer science and engineering from JSS Academy of Technical Education, India. He is a full-stack web developer with experience in major server-side web development stack (ASP.NET and Node.js) and advanced knowledge of HTML, CSS and JavaScript.

Yogesh is enthusiastic about JavaScript, and its library and framework (Backbone, AngularJS, jQuery, and Underscore).

He started his career in data mining and data warehousing, with expert level knowledge in database development. He is a Microsoft Certified Solutions Associate (MCSA) in MSSQL.

He is a self-learner and enjoys learning algorithms and data structure. He achieved a statement of accomplishment from Standford University (Coursera) for algorithms.

Currently, he is working at Gainsight as a full-stack developer. Previously, he worked at OLX India and MAQ Software.

In his spare time, he likes to blog at http://mylearning.in. His LinkedIn profile can be found at https://www.linkedin.com/in/yogesh21

I would like to thank my family, friends, and colleagues for their support.

Nikolay Sokolov is a software engineer with vast experience in cloud computing, deployment automation, and enterprise software development. Currently, he is working on core platform development at Tonomi (http://tonomi.com/), delivering the autonomic management of cloud applications based on the flexible component model.

Feel free to contact him at https://twitter.com/chemikadze

Serkan Yersen is a software developer from San Francisco. He is the author of open source libraries such as ifvisible.js, underscore.py, and kwargs.js. Serkan has specialized in building large-scale JavaScript applications and creating UIs that will be used by a large variety of users. From 2006 to 2012, Serkan worked for http://www.jotform.com/ and built a complex form builder, which is being used by millions of users. Right now, he is building web applications for Home Depot and Redbeacon (http://www.redbeacon.com/). You can reach him at http://serkan.io/.

www.PacktPub.com

Support files, eBooks, discount offers, and more

For support files and downloads related to your book, please visit www.PacktPub.com.

Did you know that Packt offers eBook versions of every book published, with PDF and ePub files available? You can upgrade to the eBook version at www.PacktPub.com and as a print book customer, you are entitled to a discount on the eBook copy. Get in touch with us at service@packtpub.com for more details.

At www.PacktPub.com, you can also read a collection of free technical articles, sign up for a range of free newsletters and receive exclusive discounts and offers on Packt books and eBooks.

https://www2.packtpub.com/books/subscription/packtlib

Do you need instant solutions to your IT questions? PacktLib is Packt's online digital book library. Here, you can search, access, and read Packt's entire library of books.

Why subscribe?

- Fully searchable across every book published by Packt
- Copy and paste, print, and bookmark content
- On demand and accessible via a web browser

Free access for Packt account holders

If you have an account with Packt at www.PacktPub.com, you can use this to access PacktLib today and view 9 entirely free books. Simply use your login credentials for immediate access.

This book is for Melissa, Jason, and Simon. Thanks for all the love and support.

Table of Contents

Preface

Some applications just get it right. These are the exceptions rather than the rule. Lots of JavaScript applications get one or two things right, and other things very wrong. The things we get wrong are a side effect of the scaling influencers that we never considered. This is a book about scaling our frontend architectures to meet the quality requirements asked of us. Scaling JavaScript applications is an interesting and fun problem. There're so many moving parts—the users, the developers, the deployment environments, the browser environments, and the task of bringing all of these factors together to form a meaningful user experience. What are we scaling, and why? The aim of this book is to help us answer these questions.

What this book covers

Chapter 1, *Scale from a JavaScript Perspective*, introduces the idea of scalable JavaScript applications and what makes them different from other applications that scale.

Chapter 2, *Influencers of Scale*, helps us understand that the need to scale helps us design better architectures.

Chapter 3, *Component Composition*, explains how the patterns that form the core of our architecture serve as blueprints for assembling components.

Chapter 4, *Component Communication and Responsibilities*, explains how components that communicate with one another are a scaling constraint. It tells us how features are the result of component communication patterns.

Chapter 5, *Addressability and Navigation*, elaborates on large-scale web applications with URIs that point to resources, and how designs that scale can handle a growing number of URIs.

Chapter 6, User Preferences and Defaults, tells us why users need control over certain aspects of our software. And it also explains that scalable application components are configurable.

Chapter 7, Load Time and Responsiveness, explains how more moving parts means performance degradation across the application. This includes making trade-offs that keep our UI responsive, while adding new features.

Chapter 8, Portability and Testing, covers writing JavaScript code that's not tightly coupled with a single environment. This includes creating portable mock data and portable tests.

Chapter 9, Scaling Down, explains how removing unused or buggy components from applications is essential, if we want to scale up in other areas.

Chapter 10, Coping with Failure, explains that large-scale JavaScript architectures can't fall over as a result of a bug in one component. This includes how designing with failure in mind is the key to achieving scale in a broad number of scenarios.

What you need for this book

- NodeJS
- Code Editor/IDE
- A modern Web browser

Who this book is for

This book is intended for a senior JavaScript developer who is curious about architectural issues in the frontend. There's no prerequisite framework knowledge required, however, most of the concepts presented throughout the book are adaptations of components found in frameworks such as Backbone, Angular, or Ember. Strong JavaScript language skills are required, and all code examples are presented using ECMAScript 6 syntax.

Conventions

In this book, you will find a number of text styles that distinguish between different kinds of information. Here are some examples of these styles and an explanation of their meaning.

Code words in text, database table names, folder names, filenames, file extensions, pathnames, dummy URLs, user input, and Twitter handles are shown as follows: " For example, `users/31729`. Here, the router will need to find a pattern that matches this string, and the pattern will also specify how to extract the `31729` variable."

A block of code is set as follows:

```
// Renders the sections of the view. Each section
    // either has a renderer, or it doesn't. Either way,
    // content is returned.
    render() {
```

> Warnings or important notes appear in a box like this.

> Tips and tricks appear like this.

Reader feedback

Feedback from our readers is always welcome. Let us know what you think about this book—what you liked or disliked. Reader feedback is important for us as it helps us develop titles that you will really get the most out of.

To send us general feedback, simply e-mail `feedback@packtpub.com`, and mention the book's title in the subject of your message.

If there is a topic that you have expertise in and you are interested in either writing or contributing to a book, see our author guide at `www.packtpub.com/authors`.

Customer support

Now that you are the proud owner of a Packt book, we have a number of things to help you to get the most from your purchase.

Downloading the example code

You can download the example code files from your account at `http://www.packtpub.com` for all the Packt Publishing books you have purchased. If you purchased this book elsewhere, you can visit `http://www.packtpub.com/support` and register to have the files e-mailed directly to you.

Errata

Although we have taken every care to ensure the accuracy of our content, mistakes do happen. If you find a mistake in one of our books — maybe a mistake in the text or the code — we would be grateful if you could report this to us. By doing so, you can save other readers from frustration and help us improve subsequent versions of this book. If you find any errata, please report them by visiting `http://www.packtpub.com/submit-errata`, selecting your book, clicking on the **Errata Submission Form** link, and entering the details of your errata. Once your errata are verified, your submission will be accepted and the errata will be uploaded to our website or added to any list of existing errata under the Errata section of that title.

To view the previously submitted errata, go to `https://www.packtpub.com/books/content/support` and enter the name of the book in the search field. The required information will appear under the **Errata** section.

Piracy

Piracy of copyrighted material on the Internet is an ongoing problem across all media. At Packt, we take the protection of our copyright and licenses very seriously. If you come across any illegal copies of our works in any form on the Internet, please provide us with the location address or website name immediately so that we can pursue a remedy.

Please contact us at `copyright@packtpub.com` with a link to the suspected pirated material.

We appreciate your help in protecting our authors and our ability to bring you valuable content.

Questions

If you have a problem with any aspect of this book, you can contact us at `questions@packtpub.com`, and we will do our best to address the problem.

1
Scale from a JavaScript Perspective

JavaScript applications are getting bigger. That's because we can do more with the language—more than most thought possible. After all, JavaScript was conceived as a means to activate otherwise static web pages. A means by which to fill gaps in HTML, as it were. Year after year, more and more web sites started developing JavaScript code to improve the functionality of their pages.

Despite the frustrations of certain language idiosyncrasies, JavaScript popularity gained critical mass—today it's the most popular programming language on GitHub (`http://githut.info/`). From then onward, web sites started looking more like applications that a user would install on their desktop. Libraries and frameworks started popping up left right and center. Why? Because frontend JavaScript applications are large and complex.

In the present day frontend development profession, there's a lot of tools at our disposal. The JavaScript language has evolved into something that's usable on its own; it's becoming less dependent on libraries to perform the most fundamental and basic programming tasks. This is especially true of the next iteration of the ECMAScript specification, where problems that have plagued developers for years are at least partially addressed by constructs added to the language. This, of course, doesn't negate the need for application frameworks. The frontend development environment and its supporting web standards are far from perfect, but they're improving.

Something that's been missing from the frontend development picture for a long time is architecture. Frontend architectures have become prevalent in recent years due to the complexity of what's being implemented. Sophisticated tools, allow frontend developers to design an architecture that's able to scale with the problems we're trying to solve. And that's the crux of this book—JavaScript architectures that scale. But scale to what exactly? It's not your traditional scaling problem in computing, where you need to handle more load in a distributed server environment. Scaling in the frontend presents its own unique challenges and constraints. This chapter will define some of the scaling issues faced by JavaScript architectures.

Scaling influencers

We don't scale our software systems just because we can. While it's common to tout scalability, these claims need to be put into practice. In order to do so, there has to be a reason for scalable software. If there's no need to scale, then it's much easier, not to mention cost-effective, to simply build a system that doesn't scale. Putting something that was built to handle a wide variety of scaling issues into a context where scale isn't warranted just feels clunky. Especially to the end user.

So we, as JavaScript developers and architects, need to acknowledge and understand the influences that necessitate scalability. While it's true that not all JavaScript applications need to scale, it may not always be the case. For example, it's difficult to say that we know this system isn't going to need to scale in any meaningful way, so let's not invest the time and effort to make it scalable. Unless we're developing a throw-away system, there's always going to be expectations of growth and success.

At the opposite end of the spectrum, JavaScript applications aren't born as mature scalable systems. They grow up, accumulating scalable properties along the way. Scaling influencers are an effective tool for those of us working on JavaScript projects. We don't want to over-engineer something straight from inception, and we don't want to build something that's tied-down by early decisions, limiting its ability to scale.

The need for scale

Scaling software is a reactive event. Thinking about scaling influencers helps us proactively prepare for these scaling events. In other systems, such as web application backends, these scaling events may be brief spikes, and are generally handled automatically. For example, there's an increased load due to more users issuing more requests. The load balancer kicks in and distributes the load evenly across backend servers. In the extreme case, the system may automatically provision new backend resources when needed, and destroy them when they're no longer of use.

Scaling events in the frontend aren't like that. Rather, the scaling events that take place generally happen over longer periods of time, and are more complex. The unique aspect of JavaScript applications is that the only hardware resources available to them are those available to the browser in which they run. They get their data from the backend, and this may scale up perfectly fine, but that's not what we're concerned with. As our software grows, a necessary side-effect of doing something successfully, is that we need to pay attention to the influencers of scale.

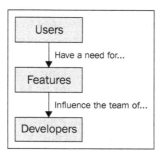

The preceding figure shows us a top-down flow chart of scaling influencers, starting with users, who require that our software implements features. Depending on various aspects of the features, such as their size and how they relate to other features, this influences the team of developers working on features. As we move down through the scaling influencers, this grows.

Growing user base

We're not building an application for just one user. If we were, there would be no need to scale our efforts. While what we build might be based on the requirements of one user representative, our software serves the needs of many users. We need to anticipate a growing user base as our application evolves. There's no exact target user count, although, depending on the nature of our application, we may set goals for the number of active users, possibly by benchmarking similar applications using a tool such as http://www.alexa.com/. For example, if our application is exposed on the public internet, we want lots of registered users. On the other hand, we might target private installations, and there, the number of users joining the system is a little slower. But even in the latter case, we still want the number of deployments to go up, increasing the total number of people using our software.

The number of users interacting with our frontend is the largest influencer of scale. With each user added, along with the various architectural perspectives, growth happens exponentially. If you look at it from a top-down point of view, users call the shots. At the end of the day, our application exists to serve them. The better we're able to scale our JavaScript code, the more users we'll please.

Building new features

Perhaps the most obvious side-effect of successful software with a strong user base is the features necessary to keep those users happy. The feature set grows along with the users of the system. This is often overlooked by projects, despite the obviousness of new features. We know they're coming, yet, little thought goes into how the endless stream of features going into our code impedes our ability to scale up our efforts.

This is especially tricky when the software is in its infancy. The organization developing the software will bend over backwards to reel in new users. And there's little consequence of doing so in the beginning because the side-effects are limited. There's not a lot of mature features, there's not a huge development team, and there's less chance of annoying existing users by breaking something that they've come to rely on. When these factors aren't there, it's easier for us to nimbly crank out the features and dazzle existing/prospective users. But how do we force ourselves to be mindful of these early design decisions? How do we make sure that we don't unnecessarily limit our ability to scale the software up, in terms of supporting more features?

As we'll see throughout this book, new feature development, as well as enhancing existing features, is an ongoing issue with scalable JavaScript architecture. It's not just the number of features listed in the marketing literature of our software that we need to be concerned about . There's also the complexity of a given feature, how common our features are with one another, and how many moving parts each of these features has. If the user is the first level when looking at JavaScript architecture from a top-down perspective, each feature is the next level, and from there, it expands out into enormous complexity.

It's not just the individual users who make a given feature complex. Instead, it's a group of users that all need the same feature in order to use our software effectively. And from there, we have to start thinking about personas, or roles, and which features are available for which roles. The need for this type of organizational structure isn't made apparent till much later on in the game; after we've made decisions that make it difficult to introduce role-based feature delivery. And depending on how our software is deployed, we may have to support a variety of unique use cases. For example, if we have several large organizations as our customers, each with their own deployments, they'll likely have their own unique constraints on how users are structured. This is challenging, and our architecture needs to support the disparate needs of many organizations, if we're going to scale.

Hiring more developers

Making these features a reality requires solid JavaScript developers who know what they're doing, and if we're lucky, we'll be able to hire a team of them. The team part doesn't happen automatically. There's a level of trust and respect that needs to be established before the team members begin to actively rely on one another to crank out some awesome code. Once that starts happening, we're in good shape. Turning once again to the top-down perspective of our scaling influencers, the features we deliver can directly impact the health of our team. There's a balance that's essentially impossible to maintain, but we can at least get close. Too many features and not enough developers lead to a sense of perpetual inadequacy among team members. When there's no chance of delivering what's expected, there's not much sense in trying. On the other hand, if you have too many developers, and there's too much communication overhead due to a limited number of features, it's tough to define responsibilities. When there's no shared understanding of responsibilities, things start to break down.

It's actually easier to deal with not enough developers for the features we're trying to develop, than having too many developers. When there's a large burden of feature development, it's a good opportunity to step back and think — "what would we do differently if we had more developers?" This question usually gets skipped. We go hire more developers, and when they arrive, it's to everyone's surprise that there's no immediate improvement in feature throughput. This is why it's best to have an open development culture where there are no stupid questions, and where responsibilities are defined.

There's no one correct team structure or development methodology. The development team needs to apply itself to the issues faced by the software we're trying to deliver. The biggest hurdle is for sure the number, size, and complexity of features. So that's something we need to consider when forming our team initially, as well as when growing the team. This latter point is especially true because the team structure we used way back when the software was new isn't going to fit what we face when the features scale up.

Architectural perspectives

The preceding section was a sampling of the factors that influence scale in JavaScript applications. Starting from the top, each of these influencers affects the influencer below it. The number and nature of our users is the first and foremost influencer, and this has a direct impact on the number and nature of the features we develop. Further more, the size of the development team, and the structure of that team, are influenced by these features. Our job is to take these influencers of scale, and translate them into factors to consider from an architectural perspective:

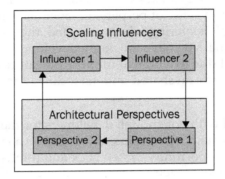

Scaling influences the perspectives of our architecture. Our architecture, in turn, determines responses to scaling influencers. The process is iterative and never-ending throughout the lifetime of our software.

The browser is a unique environment

Scaling up in the traditional sense doesn't really work in a browser environment. When backend services are overwhelmed by demand, it's common to "throw more hardware" at the problem. Easier said than done of course, but it's a lot easier to scale up our data services these days, compared to 20 years ago. Today's software systems are designed with scalability in mind. It's helpful to our frontend application if the backend services are always available and always responsive, but that's just a small portion of the issues we face.

We can't throw more hardware at the web browsers running our code; given that; the time and space complexities of our algorithms are important. Desktop applications generally have a set of system requirements for running the software, such as OS version, minimum memory, minimum CPU, and so on. If we were to advertise requirements such as these in our JavaScript applications, our user base would shrink dramatically, and possibly generate some hate mail.

The expectation that browser-based web applications be lean and fast is an emergent phenomenon. Perhaps, that's due in part to the competition we face. There are a lot of bloated applications out there, and whether they're used in the browser or natively on the desktop, users know what bloat feels like, and generally run the other way:

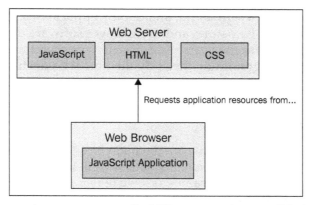

JavaScript applications require many resources, all of different types; these are all fetched by the browser, on the application's behalf.

Adding to our trouble is the fact that we're using a platform that was designed as a means to download and display hypertext, to click on a link, and repeat. Now we're doing the same thing, except with full-sized applications. Multi-page applications are slowly being set aside in favor of single-page applications. That being said, the application is still treated as though it were a web page. Despite all that, we're in the midst of big changes. The browser is a fully viable web platform, the JavaScript language is maturing, and there are numerous W3C specifications in progress; they assist with treating our JavaScript more like an application and less like a document. Take a look at the following diagram:

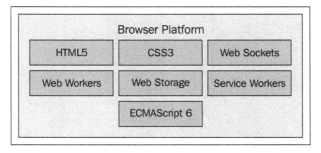

A sampling of the technologies found in the growing web platform

We use architectural perspectives to assess any architectural design we come up with. It's a powerful technique to examine our design through a different lens. JavaScript architecture is no different, especially for those that scale. The difference between JavaScript architecture and architecture for other environments is that ours have unique perspectives. The browser environment requires that we think differently about how we design, build, and deploy applications. Anything that runs in the browser is transient by nature, and this changes software design practices that we've taken for granted over the years. Additionally, we spend more time coding our architectures than diagramming them. By the time we sketch anything out, it's been superseded by another specification or another tool.

Component design

At an architectural level, components are the main building blocks we work with. These may be very high-level components with several levels of abstraction. Or, they could be something exposed by a framework we're using, as many of these tools provide their own idea of "components". For our purposes in this book, components sit somewhere in the middle—not too abstract, and not too implementation-specific. The idea being that we need to be thoughtful of our application composition, without worrying too much about the specifics.

When we first set out to build a JavaScript application with scale in mind, the composition of our components began to take shape. How our components are composed is a huge limiting factor in how we scale, because they set the standard. Components implement patterns for the sake of consistency, and it's important to get those patterns right:

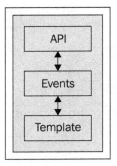

Components have an internal structure. The complexity of this composition depends on the type of component under consideration

As we'll see, the design of our various components is closely-tied to the trade-offs we make in other perspectives. And that's a good thing, because it means that if we're paying attention to the scalable qualities we're after, we can go back and adjust the design of our components in order to meet those qualities.

Component communication

Components don't sit in the browser on their own. Components communicate with one another all the time. There's a wide variety of communication techniques at our disposal here. Component communication could be as simple as method invocation, or as complex as an asynchronous publish-subscribe event system. The approach we take with our architecture depends on our more specific goals. The challenge with components is that we often don't know what the ideal communication mechanism will be, till after we've started implementing our application. We have to make sure that we can adjust the chosen communication path:

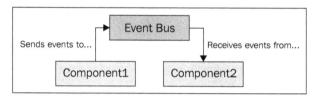

The component communication mechanism decouples components, enabling scalable structures

Seldom will we implement our own communication mechanism for our components. Not when so many tools exist, that solve at least part of the problem for us. Most likely, we'll end up with a concoction of an existing tool for communication and our own implementation specifics. What's important is that the component communication mechanism is its own perspective, which can be designed independently of the components themselves.

Load time

JavaScript applications are always loading something. The biggest challenge is the application itself, loading all the static resources it needs to run, before the user is allowed to do anything. Then there's the application data. This needs to be loaded at some point, often on demand, and contributes to the overall latency experienced by the user. Load time is an important perspective, because it hugely contributes to the overall perception of our product quality.

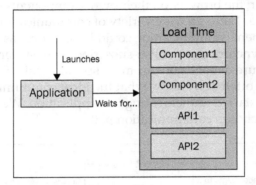

The initial load is the user's first impression and this is where most components are initialized; it's tough to get the initial load to be fast without sacrificing performance in other areas

There's lots we can do here to offset the negative user experience of waiting for things to load. This includes utilizing web specifications that allow us to treat applications and the services they use as installable components in the web browser platform. Of course, these are all nascent ideas, but worth considering as they mature alongside our application.

Responsiveness

The second part of the performance perspective of our architecture is concerned with responsiveness. That is, after everything has loaded, how long does it take for us to respond to user input? Although this is a separate problem from that of loading resources from the backend, they're still closely-related. Often, user actions trigger API requests, and the techniques we employ to handle these workflows impact user-perceived responsiveness.

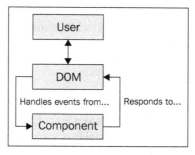

User-perceived responsiveness is affected by the time taken by our components to respond to DOM events; a lot can happen in between the initial DOM event and when we finally notify the user by updating the DOM.

Because of this necessary API interaction, user-perceived responsiveness is important. While we can't make the API go any faster, we can take steps to ensure that the user always has feedback from the UI and that feedback is immediate. Then, there's the responsiveness of simply navigating around the UI, using cached data that's already been loaded, for example. Every other architectural perspective is closely-tied to the performance of our JavaScript code, and ultimately, to the user-perceived responsiveness. This perspective is a subtle sanity-check for the design of our components and their chosen communication paths.

Addressability

Just because we're building a single-page application doesn't mean we no longer care about addressable URIs. This is perhaps the crowning achievement of the web— unique identifiers that point to the resource we want. We paste them in to our browser address bar and watch the magic happen. Our application most certainly has addressable resources, we just point to them differently. Instead of a URI that's parsed by the backend web server, where the page is constructed and sent back to the browser, it's our local JavaScript code that understands the URI:

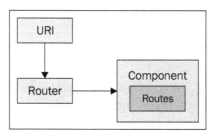

Components listen to routers for route events and respond accordingly. A changing browser URI triggers these events.

Typically, these URIs will map to an API resource. When the user hits one of these URIs in our application, we'll translate the URI into another URI that's used to request backend data. The component we use to manage these application URIs is called a router, and there's lots of frameworks and libraries with a base implementation of a router. We'll likely use one of these.

The addressability perspective plays a major role in our architecture, because ensuring that the various aspects of our application have an addressable URI complicates our design. However, it can also make things easier if we're clever about it. We can have our components utilize the URIs in the same way a user utilizes links.

Configurability

Rarely does software do what you need it to straight out of the box. Highly-configurable software systems are touted as being good software systems. Configuration in the frontend is a challenge because there's several dimensions of configuration, not to mention the issue of where we store these configuration options. Default values for configurable components are problematic too — where do they come from? For example, is there a default language setting that's set until the user changes it? As is often the case, different deployments of our frontend will require different default values for these settings:

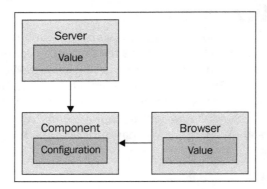

Component configuration values can come from the backend server, or from the web browser. Defaults must reside somewhere

Every configurable aspect of our software complicates its design. Not to mention the performance overhead and potential bugs. So, configurability is a large issue, and it's worth the time spent up-front discussing with various stakeholders what they value in terms of configurability. Depending on the nature of our deployment, users may value portability with their configuration. This means that their values need to be stored in the backend, under their account settings. Obviously decisions like these have backend design implications, and sometimes it's better to get away with approaches that don't require a modified backend service.

Making architectural trade-offs

There's a lot to consider from the various perspectives of our architecture, if we're going to build something that scales. We'll never get everything that we need out of every perspective simultaneously. This is why we make architectural trade-offs — we trade one aspect of our design for another more desirable aspect.

Defining your constants

Before we start making trade-offs, it's important to state explicitly what cannot be traded. What aspects of our design are so crucial to achieving scale that they must remain constant? For instance, a constant might be the number of entities rendered on a given page, or a maximum level of function call **indirection**. There shouldn't be a ton of these architectural constants, but they do exist. It's best if we keep them narrow in scope and limited in number. If we have too many strict design principles that cannot be violated or otherwise changed to fit our needs, we won't be able to easily adapt to changing influencers of scale.

Does it make sense to have constant design principles that never change, given the unpredictability of scaling influencers? It does, but only once they emerge and are obvious. So this may not be an up-front principle, though we'll often have at least one or two up-front principles to follow. The discovery of these principles may result from the early refactoring of code or the later success of our software. In any case, the constants we use going forward must be made explicit and be agreed upon by all those involved.

Performance for ease of development

Performance bottlenecks need to be fixed, or avoided in the first place where possible. Some performance bottlenecks are obvious and have an observable impact on the user experience. These need to be fixed immediately, because it means our code isn't scaling for some reason, and might even point to a larger design issue.

Other performance issues are relatively small. These are generally noticed by developers running benchmarks against code, trying by all means necessary to improve the performance. This doesn't scale well, because these smaller performance bottlenecks that aren't observable by the end user are time-consuming to fix. If our application is of a reasonable size, with more than a few developers working on it, we're not going to be able to keep up with feature development if everyone's fixing minor performance problems.

These micro-optimizations introduce specialized solutions into our code, and they're not exactly easy reading for other developers. On the other hand, if we let these minor inefficiencies go, we will manage to keep our code cleaner and thus easier to work with. Where possible, trade off optimized performance for better code quality. This improves our ability to scale from a number of perspectives.

Configurability for performance

It's nice to have generic components where nearly every aspect is configurable. However, this approach to component design comes at a performance cost. It's not noticeable at first, when there are few components, but as our software scales in feature count, the number of components grows, and so does the number of configuration options. Depending on the size of each component (its complexity, number of configuration options, and so forth) the potential for performance degradation increases exponentially. Take a look at the following diagram:

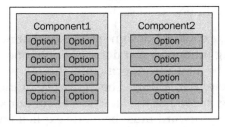

The component on the left has twice as many configuration options as the component on the right. It's also twice as difficult to use and maintain.

We can keep our configuration options around as long as there're no performance issues affecting our users. Just keep in mind that we may have to remove certain options in an effort to remove performance bottlenecks. It's unlikely that configurability is going to be our main source of performance issues. It's also easy to get carried away as we scale and add features. We'll find, retrospectively, that we created configuration options at design time that we thought would be helpful, but turned out to be nothing but overhead. Trade off configurability for performance when there's no tangible benefit to having the configuration option.

Performance for substitutability

A related problem to that of configurability is substitutability. Our user interface performs well, but as our user base grows and more features are added, we discover that certain components cannot be easily substituted with another. This can be a developmental problem, where we want to design a new component to replace something pre-existing. Or perhaps we need to substitute components at runtime.

Our ability to substitute components lies mostly with the component communication model. If the new component is able to send/receive messages/events the same as the existing component, then it's a fairly straightforward substitution. However, not all aspects of our software are substitutable. In the interest of performance, there may not even be a component to replace.

As we scale, we may need to re-factor larger components into smaller components that are replaceable. By doing so, we're introducing a new level of indirection, and a performance hit. Trade off minor performance penalties to gain substitutability that aids in other aspects of scaling our architecture.

Ease of development for addressability

Assigning addressable URIs to resources in our application certainly makes implementing features more difficult. Do we actually need URIs for every resource exposed by our application? Probably not. For the sake of consistency though, it would make sense to have URIs for almost every resource. If we don't have a router and URI generation scheme that's consistent and easy to follow, we're more likely to skip implementing URIs for certain resources.

It's almost always better to have the added burden of assigning URIs to every resource in our application than to skip out on URIs. Or worse still, not supporting addressable resources at all. URIs make our application behave like the rest of the Web; the training ground for all our users. For example, perhaps URI generation and routes are a constant for anything in our application—a trade-off that cannot happen. Trade off ease of development for addressability in almost every case. The ease of development problem with regard to URIs can be tackled in more depth as the software matures.

Maintainability for performance

The ease with which features are developed in our software boils down to the development team and it's scaling influencers. For example, we could face pressure to hire entry-level developers for budgetary reasons. How well this approach scales depends on our code. When we're concerned with performance, we're likely to introduce all kinds of intimidating code that relatively inexperienced developers will have trouble swallowing. Obviously, this impedes the ease of developing new features, and if it's difficult, it takes longer. This obviously does not scale with respect to customer demand.

Developers don't always have to struggle with understanding the unorthodox approaches we've taken to tackle performance bottlenecks in specific areas of the code. We can certainly help the situation by writing quality code that's understandable. Maybe even documentation. But we won't get all of this for free; if we're to support the team as a whole as it scales, we need to pay the productivity penalty in the short term for having to coach and mentor.

Trade off ease of development for performance in critical code paths that are heavily utilized and not modified often. We can't always escape the ugliness required for performance purposes, but if it's well-hidden, we'll gain the benefit of the more common code being comprehensible and self-explanatory. For example, low-level JavaScript libraries perform well and have a cohesive API that's easy to use. But if you look at some of the underlying code, it isn't pretty. That's our gain — having someone else maintain code that's ugly for performance reasons.

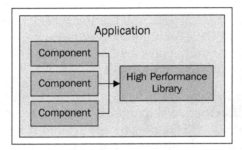

Our components on the left follow coding styles that are consistent and easy to read; they all utilize the high-performance library on the right, giving our application performance while isolating optimized code that's difficult to read and understand.

Less features for maintainability

When all else fails, we need to take a step back and look holistically at the featureset of our application. Can our architecture support them all? Is there a better alternative? Scrapping an architecture that we've sunk many hours into almost never makes sense — but it does happen. The majority of the time, however, we'll be asked to introduce a challenging set of features that violate one or more of our architectural constants.

When that happens, we're disrupting stable features that already exist, or we're introducing something of poor quality into the application. Neither case is good, and it's worth the time, the headache, and the cursing to work with the stakeholders to figure out what has to go.

If we've taken the time to figure out our architecture by making trade-offs, we should have a sound argument for why our software can't support hundreds of features.

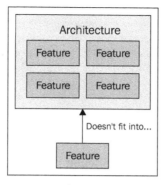

When an architecture is full, we can't continue to scale. The key is understanding where that breaking threshold lies, so we can better understand and communicate it to stakeholders.

Leveraging frameworks

Frameworks exist to help us implement our architecture using a cohesive set of patterns. There's a lot of variety out there, and choosing which framework is a combination of personal taste, and fitness based on our design. For example, one JavaScript application framework will do a lot for us out-of-the-box, while another has even more features, but a lot of them we don't need.

JavaScript application frameworks vary in size and sophistication. Some come with batteries included, and some tend toward mechanism over policy. None of these frameworks were specifically designed for our application. Any purported ability of a framework needs to be taken with a grain of salt. The features advertised by frameworks are applied to a general case, and a simple one at that. Applied in the context of our architecture is something else entirely.

That being said, we can certainly use a given framework of our liking as input to the design process. If we really like the tool, and our team has experience using it, we can let it influence our design decisions. Just as long as we understand that the framework does not automatically respond to scaling influencers—that part is up to us.

It's worth the time investigating the framework to use for our project because choosing the wrong framework is a costly mistake. The realization that we should have gone with something else usually comes after we've implemented lots of functionality. The end result is lots of re-writing, re-planning, re-training, and re-documenting. Not to mention the time lost on the first implementation. Choose your frameworks wisely, and be cautious about being framework-coupling.

Frameworks versus libraries

Why use a mash-up of smaller libraries when there's a monolithic framework out there with everything that we need? Libraries are our tools, and if they fulfill a need in our architecture, by all means use them. Some developers shy away from low-level tools because of the dependency-chaos that ensues. In practice, this happens anyway, even if we're leveraging an all-encompassing framework.

At the end of the day, the distinction between frameworks and libraries doesn't really matter to us. Creating a third-party dependency nightmare doesn't scale well. Neither does sticking with one tool exclusively and maintaining a lot of code ourselves. It's about finding the right fit between depending heavily on other projects and reinventing the wheel ourselves.

Implementing patterns consistently

The tools we use to help implement our architecture do so by exposing patterns common throughout JavaScript applications. And they do so consistently. As our application scales in size due to a growing featureset, we can apply the same framework components over and over. Frameworks also promote consistency in the patterns we implement ourselves. If we look at the internals of any framework, we will see that it has its own generic components; these are extended to provide us with usable components.

Performance is built in

Open source frameworks have the most developers looking at the code, and the most projects using the framework in production. They get lots of feedback from the community of users, and these include performance enhancements. Third-party tools are the right place to focus on performance, because they're likely the most utilized code in a given application. Leaving all performance outcomes up to browser vendors and JavaScript libraries isn't smart. Leveraging the performance behind components we use all the time is smart.

Leverage community wisdom

Successful JavaScript frameworks have strong communities surrounding them. This is more powerful than having robust documentation because we can ask questions as they arise. Odds are, someone else is trying to do something similar in their project, using the same framework as us. Open source projects are like a knowledge engine; even if the exact answer we need isn't out there, we can often find enough through the wisdom of the community to figure it out ourselves.

Frameworks don't scale out-of-the-box

Saying one framework scales better than another isn't justified. Writing a **TODO** application as a benchmark for how well the framework scales is hardly useful. We write TODO applications to get a feel for the framework, and how it compares to others. If we're unsure about which framework fits our style, a TODO application is a good start.

Our goal is to implement something that scales well in response to influencers. These are unique and unknown upfront. The best we can do is make predictions about what scaling influencers we'll likely be hit with in the future. Based on these likely influencers, and the nature of the application we're building, some frameworks are better candidates than others. Frameworks help us scale, but they don't scale for us.

Summary

Scaling a JavaScript application isn't the same as scaling other types of applications. Although we can use JavaScript to create large-scale backend services, our concern is with scaling the applications our users interact with in the browser. And there're a number of influencers that guide our decision making process on producing an architecture that scales.

We reviewed some of these influencers, and how they flow in a top-down fashion, creating challenges unique to frontend JavaScript development. We examined the effect of more users, more features, and more developers; we can see that there's a lot to think about. While the browser is becoming a powerful platform, onto which we're delivering our applications, it still has constraints not found on other platforms.

Designing and implementing a scalable JavaScript application requires having an architecture. What the software must ultimately do is just one input to that design. The scaling influencers are key as well. From there, we address different perspectives of the architecture under consideration. Things such as component composition and responsiveness come into play when we talk about scale. These are observable aspects of our architecture that are impacted by influencers of scale.

As these scaling factors change over time, we use architectural perspectives as tools to modify our design, or the product to align with scaling challenges. The focus of the next chapter will be to look into these scaling influencers in more detail. Understanding them and putting together a checklist will empower us to implement a JavaScript that scales in response to these events.

2
Influencers of Scale

Influencers of scale start with the users of our software. They're the number one influencer because they're the reason we've set out to build an application. As we saw in the preceding chapter, users influence features that ultimately influence the code we write and the development personnel who implement it. When we pause and think about these scaling influencers, we recognize that a sound JavaScript architecture that can handle them is a prudent cause. We can then take our findings and look at our code from different architectural perspectives. We'll dig into each of these perspectives throughout this book, starting with the next chapter.

But before we do that, let's go into more detail on these influencers of scale. We want to pay close attention to these because with every decision we make about our design, how it actually scales depends largely on the influences we've anticipated. Perhaps more importantly, we need to design our architecture in such a way that it enables us to handle scaling scenarios we haven't anticipated.

We'll start with a closer look at the users of our software. Why are they using it? How does our software make them happy? What's in it for us? These questions, believe it or not, are pertinent to the way we write our JavaScript. From users, we then move down to features, the outward-facing personality of our application. Some features aren't a good fit for our application, but sometimes that doesn't matter — we don't have a say. If we're going to scale up, to please our users, sometimes we have to make the best of these features.

The development resources, ultimately responsible for implementing these features, are a scaling influencer that can make or break a product. We'll look at the challenges faced by the development team, and how they're constrained by the feature influences. We'll close the chapter with a generic checklist for each of these influencers; to help ensure we've thought of the most pressing issues concerning our ability to scale.

Scaling users

The most important user is us — the development organization. While our mission is to keep our users happy by delivering software that scales, we need to keep ourselves happy too. And that requires a viable business model. The reason we care about this is because different models mean different approaches to acquire new users, and manage existing users. From there, the complexities of scaling our user base get deeper. We need to consider how our users are organized, how they use our software to communicate with one another, how to provide support, collect feedback, and collect user metrics.

Viable business models for JavaScript applications range from deploying a free service that's ad-supported, to a private, on-premise deployment of our software, where we collect license fees. Deciding which approach is right for the organization is likely out of our hands. However, it's our responsibility to understand the chosen business model and relate it to the current and future users of our software.

The business model can grow quite complex. For instance, organizations will often start off with one approach that's clear cut and keeps users happy, while meeting business expectations. However, as the organization grows and matures, the once coherent business model is obscured into something that's less approachable, and has unpredictable results for our architecture. Let's take a look at some of these business models and how each impacts the scalability of our user base.

License fees

Software licensing is a complex topic, one that we're not going to explore in depth here. What's important is simply whether or not we're relying on licensed software as our business model. If we are, then we likely have other organizations deploying our JavaScript applications on-premise. It's unlikely that we'll have individuals purchasing licenses. Not impossible though — it depends on the nature of the software. The likely case with selling licenses is that our software will be privately deployed by multiple organizations.

There are two interesting scaling properties to consider with this business model. Firstly, there's a fundamental limit on the number of users within a given organization. While organizations can be large, and we can sell to multiple large organizations, the common case is to have fewer users overall with a licensed model. Secondly, each organization has different needs in terms of customizations. This involves configurability, user organization, and so on. We're more likely to experience requests for these types of changes or enhancements using a licensed model.

So, while there're not as many users to support, the nature of supporting them is more complex due to the structure of the organization using our software, and hence difficult to scale. Dependency management in these environments can be challenging as well, due to restrictions that determine how our software is able to scale. In other environments, these restrictions are more lax.

Subscription fees

Subscriptions are recurring fees we collect for the use of our software. This approach costs our users less, most of the time. It's also a more flexible business model in that it can easily apply to software that's deployed on-premise, and software that's deployed publicly.

Since it's cheaper for organizations to deploy subscription-based software rather than license-based ones, we're more likely to reach more organizations. Mind you, these are organizations divided into departments, each with their own budgetary constraints.

In terms of scale, however, the challenge with subscriptions is similar to the challenge faced with licenses, that is, complex customization requests. If subscriptions are likely to get us more on-premise deployments and likely more arcane feature requests. Another scaling problem facing the subscription approach is customer retention. Users aren't going to continue paying subscription fees if value isn't continuously delivered.

So if we go the subscription route, we need to scale up our efforts in delivering new features that justify the recurring subscription costs for our users.

Consumption fees

Another business model for software is consumption, or, pay-as-you-go. This is an appealing model for users since they're not paying for resources they don't use. Of course, this doesn't suit every application. What if there are no meaningful resources for users to consume? What if we're running our application in a way that resource consumption is of no concern to us?

In other cases, the resource usage is glaringly obvious. Maybe the user performs some computationally-expensive task, or stores a lot of data for a period of time. In these cases, the consumption model makes perfect sense, for both us and the user. Users that consume less, pay less. User behavior can be erratic, with spikes of consumption. However, these events are brief, relative to the rest of the time they're using our application.

The scaling challenge we face with this business model is that we need good tools in addition to the core aspects of our application. First, we need a tool that measures and records consumption. Second, we need tools to accurately portray these consumption metrics, often visually. Depending on what users are consuming, and what level of integration we're expecting, there might be a third-party component to consider.

Ad-supported

Another option is to deploy our application to the public internet and use display advertisements for revenue. These are free applications, and hence more likely to be used. On the other hand, advertisements are a big turn-off to many people, which counteracts the appeal of "free".

Perhaps the goal when using this approach, rather than ad revenue, is generating mass usage. The two go hand-in-hand actually, more users means more ad revenue. However, mass adoption of an online JavaScript application can catch the attention of investors. So lots of user accounts, by itself, has merit.

These types of applications are different from those that follow other business models, in how they scale. Applications that gain mass appeal on the internet solve different problems for different user personas. Following this model means we need to have reach, and to scale our reach means lowering the barrier to entry. Our focus, while using this business model, is on ease-of-use and social validity.

Open source

The final business model for us to consider is open source. Don't laugh; open source software is vital to the functioning of the web. It's highly unlikely that our JavaScript application doesn't use any open source components. It's more likely that we're only using open source components. But why do people spend their valuable time developing tools for everyone else to use, even their competition?

The first misconception here is that folks are just sitting around, unemployed, building open source software for the rest of us to use. The fact is, most of the tools we'll use are built by people in strong positions at companies that use the same technologies we do. They may have even started the open source project to solve a problem for the company — to provide a missing tool in their development process.

The second misconception is that we're helping out our competitors by starting up, or contributing to, open source projects. It's not possible for us to single-handedly put ourselves in a worse position than our competition via open source software. By other measures, yes, it's absolutely possible to help out our competition by hurting ourselves.

On the other hand, open source projects can be good for an organization. They have to be effective projects; something that's usable and generic. If it grows legs, we're creating new stakeholders in technology that we rely on, and that's a good thing. The community that surrounds an open source project is invaluable. While open source by itself can't support an organization, there's no escaping the fact that it's an integral part of any JavaScript application business model.

Groups and rolesGroups allow us to classify our users. Think of the role as a user type. This is a powerful abstraction, because it allows us to generalize aspects of features by role type. For example, instead of checking conditions based on user properties, we check them based on role properties. It's a lot easier to move a user from one role to another, than to modify our logic.

Figuring out user roles and how they translate into group implementations is a tricky subject. The only thing we can count on is having to shuffle around the organizational structure of our users. So, making the grouping mechanism as generic as possible is our first goal. This has trade-offs too — anything that's completely generic has negative performance implications.

Some grouping decisions will be obvious up front. Like whether users are aware of other users in the system or not. If they are, we can start drilling into the specific questions around how users communicate with one another using our application. Again, this may be obvious based on the types of features our application has. The business model we're following influences our user management design as well. If we're selling software licenses and likely to be deployed on-premise, then we can expect lots of varying needs for user roles, and the subsequent grouping implementation. If we're deployed publicly on the internet, grouping is less of a concern — we can probably choose a simple approach in favor of performance, for example.

As our software grows more complex, as we add more features and bring on more customers, we'll start to see the need to segregate parts of our application. That is, we'll need to tie-down certain features based on access control permissions. Rather than having different user roles, install separate software systems; it's easier for them to have a single system with users, groups, and access control.

This has implications for us as JavaScript architects because once we start down the access control path, there's no turning back. From that point forward, we have to be consistent — every feature needs to check for the appropriate permissions. Further complicating matters, is that if we're grouping users this way, we're probably going to have to group other entities of our system in a similar fashion at some point. Which only makes sense, especially to the end user – this group of things is accessed and used by that group of users.

Communicating users

Another aspect to consider with regard to users, and their relationships with one another, is the communication channels available to these users. Do they explicitly pick and choose other users to communicate with? Or is the communication more implicit? An example of the latter might be a user from the same group as us, looking at a chart. This chart is generated based on data that's put into the system by other members of the group. Is it worthwhile to think about these sorts of implicit communication channels in addition to the explicit ones?

The nature of our application determines which communication channels are open to our users. It might also depend on the users themselves. Some applications have users that need to get in there, and expertly perform a task—communicating with other users is unnecessary. On the other hand, we might find ourselves developing something that's a little more social-minded. In fact, we might even depend on the services of an external social network.

If we're going to rely on third-party user management, social networks or otherwise, we have to be careful how tightly coupled we become with these services. In terms of scale, using third-party authentication mechanisms may have social bonus features we want—especially considering that most users will love the fact that they don't need yet another account to use our application. Scaling this approach to user management becomes a problem from other perspectives once we start implementing new features, where third-party integration is complex. For example, a photo editing application might scale better using a Facebook login, since that's where most users' photos originate.

Users are going to find a way to communicate with one another if our application is useful or fun to use. We can fight it, or we can leverage user communication as a tool to help us scale. That is, scale the transparency with which our users can point their peers to something useful, that they would otherwise have to go and dig-around for.

Support mechanisms

It's great to have our JavaScript application just work. Even when everything's going according to plan, we've deployed and there are no bugs, we have to support the cases where the users have no idea how to use something. Or they've performed some action they probably shouldn't have. Or where one of the other ten million usability issues are relevant, and swift rescue is in order.

Our support mechanism not scaling can grind our business to a halt. So, in addition to our software scaling well, we need to think about how the user support systems are going to scale alongside it. Support can be tightly integrated, or farmed out to third-party software and personnel.

It's better if users don't need support to use our software. That's why we design with usability in mind. We walk through the various user experiences, often with experts and/or actual users, and integrate design for them in our software. This is the most obvious thing we can tackle when it comes to supporting our users. Because if we can do this, through usability design, then we can eliminate a large portion of the likely support issues we'll face as we scale.

Regardless, we still have to assume that we're not thinking of the support cases that will inevitably pop up after deployment. Users are inquisitive. Even if everything is going fine, they still might have questions. So we can't really say, "we've designed a great user experience for you and everything's working, so go away". We need to be responsive with our users' questions and concerns. Because the second we're being dismissive about inquiries, we're failing to scale our application.

Can our JavaScript components help with supporting our users? If that's what we want, absolutely! In fact, contextual help is probably the most effective. If a user has a question about a particular component, and they see a help button, right there within the problematic component, then they can use that to submit their question. On the receiving end of the support question, there's less confusion. We know exactly what the user is trying to do, and spending time creating the context around the issue is no longer necessary.

This is definitely easier said than done and has other scaling implications for us. These contextual help systems aren't effort-free. And should we decide to go that route, we' would have to consider contextual help with every feature we implement. Can this scale alongside everything else we're doing?

Another approach we might want to consider is a knowledge base with information from the organization creating the software, and also from those that use it. Those using it for a particular purpose are apt to have better answers than us, and these answers are super-valuable. Not only to users looking for answers, but also to us.

Feedback mechanisms

Is feedback really worth differentiating from support? Support is definitely feedback. If we pay attention to the various support issues we encounter over time, we can transform it into feedback and use this information as feedback. However, it's still worth differentiating the two forms, because the user is in a different frame of mind. While experiencing a support issue, there's frustration, ranging from mild to intense. This user doesn't care about improving the product now — they need to get their job done.

On the other hand, users who've used our software for a while grow acutely aware of the inefficiencies of their workflow. Collecting this type of feedback is crucial. How do we get it? One option is supplying a feedback button in the application, as we would with a contextual support button. Another option is to let a third-party handle feedback collection. As with support, automating the context is always better for us when it comes to understanding what the user is talking about without spending too much time on it.

The key with feedback is keeping customers engaged. Not everyone who uses our software is going to share their thoughts with us. But some no doubt will—even if they're just venting frustration. We have to respond to these in order to establish a dialog. Users who supply feedback like this want us to respond to them. And it's in the ongoing conversation with these users where the product improvements emerge, not in the brilliant ideas initially submitted by users.

As our user base grows, can we keep up and stay responsive to user feedback? Obviously this is a challenge, given everything else that's on our plate, dealing with our application's growth. It's one thing to create dialog around a given piece of user data, but it's another to act on that feedback. Suppose we've enabled great feedback mechanisms, embedded in our software. We will have to turn this into actionable work at some point. So, we need to think about how our process of generating requirements based on user feedback scales. If it doesn't, and user feedback is never acted upon, they'll bail and we will have failed to scale.

Notifying users

JavaScript applications need to display notifications to its users. These can be fairly straightforward to implement, especially if we're mainly concerned with responding to user actions. For example, when users do something, it results in an API request to the back-end. We will want to display a notification to the user, indicating that the action has succeeded or failed. These notifications look the same across the application—we can use the same tool for most, if not all, notifications.

Notifications are easy to forget about in terms of designing a scalable JavaScript architecture. It's a big topic—there are contextual notifications, general notifications, and notifications that take place when the user is offline. The latter generally means that something has been emailed to the user, prompting them to log in and take action if need be.

The contextual notifications are probably the most important, as they supply feedback to the user on something they're currently doing. This is challenging to scale because we have to ensure that these types of notifications remain consistent across the user interface, for all types of entities. The more general notifications take place as a result of something happening in the background.

Some resource that belongs to a user may have changed state, either expectedly or unexpectedly. Regardless, the user probably wants to know about these events. Ideally, if they're logged in and using the system, then a generic notification will reveal itself. However, we may want these types of notifications emailed to users as well.

The challenge with any notification system is volume. If there are a lot of users, and they're fairly active, a lot of notifications will need to be generated and delivered. This will no doubt interfere with the performance of other components in our code. We're also faced with the configurability that comes with notifications. We'll never get the notifications right for all of our users, so we'll need some degree of notification tuning. The right level that scales our application is up to us JavaScript architects and developers.

User metrics

The best way to approach the question of how users interact with our software is through data. Certain data points cannot be guessed at or manually collected. This is where we need to rely on tools that automatically collect user metrics as they interact with our software. With the raw data in place, we're well-equipped to analyze what we see, and make decisions.

While it makes sense to automate this task, the task may not be necessary in the first place. It may only be worthwhile to collect user metrics when we're really unsure about the future direction of a given feature, or when we want further insight on what work to prioritize. A lot of the time, we can get these answers without much effort, and 'there'll certainly be no need for analytical tools. We may not even be permitted to collect such data if we've deployed on-premise somewhere.

There's a ton of good third-party metric collection tools available. These are especially helpful because they ship with a lot of the reporting we need. And a lot that we don't. There's also the question of how tightly integrated we want our third-party components. There's always a chance that we would need to turn such a feature off. Or, at least change where such data is stored.

There are a number of uses for this data other than just input for product direction decisions. Our code can take user metric data and reflectively improve the experience. This could be something as innocent as making suggestions on what to do next, based on past events. Or we could get really fancy and make efficiency optimizations based on this data. It all comes down to the common case of what our users want. Figuring out what our users want is a scaling problem in and of itself, because as we grow, we acquire more users who all want different things. User metrics could turn out to be a helpful tool with which to combat this issue.

Scaling users example

Our software firm is developing an online lending application. It's fairly straightforward; there's not a lot of moving parts in the front end. The applicant first creates an account, and then can apply for a new loan and manage existing loans. The business model of this application is consumption-based. We earn revenue through interest on the loans, so the more the loans consumed, the more we earn.

The obvious scaling influencers are user volume and ease of use. Part of our value proposition is low interest on small loans. There should be very little overhead for the users when applying for a new loan; minimal input required, and minimal wait time for the loan application to succeed or fail. This is our highly focused vision for delivering value, and some of more apparent scaling influencers we'll be up against.

Let's think about some of the more subtle implications of our application with regard to scale. Given the type of application this is, we're unlikely to see requests for social functions. For the most part, the user can be treated as a black box; they're in their own little universe when using our application. Since ease of use is very important to us, and our application has few moving parts, support and feedback are unlikely factors when it comes to scale. We can't eliminate support and feedback, but our focus on those areas can be minimal.

On the other hand, we need to market our service and we really have no idea what our customers are getting loans for, what are the most popular repayment schedules, and so on. For this, we can probably deliver a more effective market message, as well as improve our overall user experience. The implication here being that collecting meta data about our application is a big deal. Since we're after large user numbers, the implication is that we'll need to store lots of meta data. We'll also have to design each feature in such a way that we can collect metrics and store them for later use, which complicates the design.

Scaling features

Now we'll turn our attention to scaling the features we implement in our software. The users are the ultimate influence, and now that we have a rough idea of what's required in terms of scaling them, we can put this knowledge to work with feature development. When we think about scaling users, we're thinking about the why. Why do we choose this business model over that business model? Why do we need to enable things for one user role, and disable them for others? Once we get into actually designing and implementing the feature in JavaScript, we start thinking of the how. Not only are we concerned about correctness, but also scalability. As with users, influencers are the determinant when it comes to scalable features.

Application value

We'd like to think that we're doing a good job with the features we implement, and that with each new feature we introduce, we're providing value to the user. It's worthwhile for us to think about this, because in essence, that's what we're trying to do—scale the value of our software to a broader audience. An example of not scaling, in this regard, is when existing users who rely on existing features are neglected, and feel disappointed with our software because we've focused on scaling new areas.

This happens when we forget about the problems we had originally set out to solve with our software. It might sound like a ridiculous notion, but it's easy to move in a completely different direction based on a number of factors. In some rare cases, this change in direction has led to some of the most successful software the world has seen. In the more common case, it leads to failed software, and it is indeed a scaling problem. There's a core set of value propositions our software should always deliver—this is the essence of our software and should never falter. We're often faced with other scaling influencers, like the addition of new customers who want different things from the core values offered by our software. The inability to handle this means we're not able to scale the main value proposition of our application.

An indicator that we're headed down the wrong path when it comes to scaling value is confusion with current value and ideal value. That is, what our software currently does versus what we might like it to do someday. We have to be forward thinking, there's no doubt about that. But future plans need to be continuously sanity-checked against what's possible. And this often means backtracking to why we set out to create the software in the first place.

If our application is really compelling, and we hope that it is, then we have to fight against other scaling influencers to keep it that way. Maybe this means that part of our process for evaluating new features involves ensuring the feature in some way contributes to the core value proposition features of our software. Not all features under consideration will be able to, and these deserve the most scrutiny. Is it really worth the change in direction, and jeopardy to our ability to scale?

Killer features versus features that kill

We want our application to stand out from the crowd. It'd be nice if there were a niche-enough market where we had little to no competition. Then it would be easy to implement stable software that just works, without anything fancy, and everyone would be happy. Given that this isn't reality, we have to differentiate—one such way to do this is by implementing a killer feature—which is an aspect of our software that nobody else has, and something users care deeply for.

The challenge is that killer features are rarely planned. Instead, they're a side-effect of something else going well in the delivery of our application. As we continuously mature our application, refining and tweaking features, we'll stumble upon that one "minor" change that evolves into a killer feature. It's no surprise that this is often the way killer features come into being. By listening to our customers and meeting scaling requirements, we're able to evolve our features. We add new features, take some away, and modify existing features. If we do that successfully for long enough, the killer features will reveal themselves.

Sometimes it's clear during the planning of a given feature that it's trying to be a killer feature, for the sake of being a killer feature. That's not optimal. Nor is it valuable to the user. They didn't choose our software because we had "lots of killer features" on our product roadmap. They chose us because we do something they need done. Possibly more efficiently than the alternatives. As we start thinking about killer features for their own sake, we start gravitating away from the core values of our application.

The best solution to this problem is an open environment, one that welcomes input from all team members at feature inception time. The earlier we're able to kill a bad idea, the more time we will save by not working on it. It's not always as clear-cut as this, unfortunately, and we have to do some development on the feature in order to discover that one or more aspects don't scale well. This could be for any number of reasons, but it's not a total loss. If we're still willing to pull the plug on a feature after development has commenced, then we can learn a valuable lesson.

When things don't scale and we decide to terminate the feature, we'll be doing our software a favor. We're not compromising our architecture by forcing something on it that doesn't work. We'll reach a point during the development of any feature where we'll need to ask ourselves; "do we value this feature more than the architecture we have in place, and if so, are we willing to change the architecture to accommodate it?" Most of the time, our architecture is more valuable than the feature. So putting a stop to developing something that doesn't fit can serve as a valuable lesson. In the future, we'll have a better idea of what will scale and what won't, based on this cancelled feature.

Data-driven features

It's one thing to have an application with a large and varied user base. It's another to be able to make use of the ways they interact with our software by collecting data. User metrics are a powerful tool for collecting information pertinent to making decisions about our software, and the future direction it takes. We'll call these data-driven features.

In the beginning, when we have few or no users, we obviously can't collect user metrics. We'll have to rely on other information, such as the collective wisdom of our team. We've all likely worked on JavaScript projects in the past, so we have enough of a rough idea to get the product off the ground. Once there, we need tools in place to better support our decisions on features. In particular, which features we need versus those that we do not? As our software matures, and we collect more user metrics, we can further refine our features to match the reality of what our users need.

Having the necessary data to make a feature data-driven is a challenging feat to scale, because we need the mechanism to collect and refine the data in the first place. This requires development effort that we simply may not have. Additionally, we have to actually make the decisions about features based on this data—the data alone isn't going to turn itself into requirements for us.

We'll also want to predict the viability of features we've been asked to implement. This task is difficult without data to support our hypotheses. For example, do we have any data on the environments in which our application will run? Simple data points can be enough to determine that a feature isn't worth implementing.

Data-driven features work from two angles, that is, the data we collect automatically, and the data we supply. Both are difficult to scale, and yet both are necessary to scale. The only real solution is to make sure that the number of features we implement are small enough in number, so that we can handle the amount of data generated by a given feature.

Competing with other products

Unless we're operating in a completely niche market, there's a good probability of competing products. Even if we are in a somewhat niche market, there's still going to be some overlap with other applications. There're a lot of software development firms out there— so we're likely to face direct competition. We compete with similar offerings by creating superior features. This means that not only do we have to keep delivering top-notch software, but we need to be aware of what the competition is up to, and what users of their software think. This is a limiting factor in our ability to scale, because we have to spend time understanding how these competing technologies work.

If we have a sales force out-selling our product, they're often a good source of information on what the other guys are doing. They'll often be asked by prospective customers if our software does such and such because this other application does it. Perhaps the most compelling selling point is that we can deliver that feature, and we can do it better.

This is where we must be careful, as this is yet another scaling factor that limits our ability to win customers. We have to scale to promises we make to existing and prospective customers. Promise too much, and we won't be able to implement the features, leading to disappointed users. Promise too little, or nothing at all, and we won't win customers in the first place. The best way to combat this scaling limitation is to ensure that those selling our product are kept well in touch with the reality of our software. What it can and cannot do, what's a future possibility versus impractical options.

To sell our product, there has to be some wiggle room for promising some things without understanding the full implications of implementing such promises. Otherwise, we won't get the customers we're after, because we're not generating any excitement around our product. If we're going to scale this approach to selling to new customers, we need a proven means to distill the promises into something that's achievable. On the one hand, we can't compromise the architecture. On the other hand, we have to meet somewhere in the middle to give the user what they need.

Modifying existing features

Long after we've successfully deployed our JavaScript application, we're still constantly refining the design of our code and the overall architecture. The only constant is change, or something to that effect. It takes a sizeable amount of discipline to go back and modify existing features of our software in an effort to improve the experience for users. The reason is that we feel more pressure from stakeholders to add new features. This presents a long-term scaling problem for our application because we can't add new features forever, without ever improving what's already in place.

The unlikely scenario is that there's no need to change anything; all our existing users are happy and they don't want us to touch anything. Some users are afraid of change, which means they like aspects of our software because we did a good job implementing them. We obviously want more features that are this good, by which, users are generally happy and don't see a need to improve.

So how do we reach this point? We have to listen to user feedback, and base our roadmap for modifying features on this feedback. To keep scaling along with our users and their demands, we have to strike a balance between implementing new features and modifying existing features. One way to check if we're moving in the right direction with feature enhancements is to broadcast the proposed changes to our user base. We can then gauge the feedback we get, if any. In fact, this might entice our otherwise quiet users to give us some specific suggestions. It's a way of putting the ball in the user's court—"here's what we're thinking, what do you think?"

Beyond figuring out what features to improve and when to improve them relative to implementing new features, there's the architectural risk. How tightly coupled is our code? Can we isolate a feature to the extent that there's no chance of us breaking other features? We're never going to completely eliminate this risk—we can only reduce coupling. The scaling issue at play here is how much time do we spend modifying a given feature due to re-factoring, fixing regressions, and so on? We spend less time on these activities when our components are loosely-coupled, consequently, we can scale our feature enhancements. From a management point of view, we always run the risk of blocking other people in the organization, through conflicts brought about by our changes.

Supporting user groups and roles

Depending on the type of business model we're following and the size of our user base, user management becomes a scaling issue for us because it touches every feature we implement. This is further complicated by the fact that the user management is likely to change just as frequently as the feature requirements are. As our application grows, we'll likely be dealing with roles, groups, and access control.

There are a lot of side-effects with complicated user management. The new feature we've just implemented may work perfectly fine initially, but fail in a number of other scenarios our production customers are likely to face. This means that we need more time dedicated to testing features, and the quality assurance team is probably already overwhelmed. Not to mention the additional security and privacy implications that arise from complicated user management in each of our features.

We can't really do much about complex user management schemas, as they're often symptomatic of the organization using the application, and its structure. We're more likely to face these types of complexities with on-premise deployments.

Introducing new services

There comes a point where the current back-end services no longer suffice for new features. We can scale our front-end development efforts better when there's very little dependency on the back-end. If that sounds counter-intuitive, don't worry. It's true that we need back-end services to carry out the requests of our users. So the dependency will always be there. What we want to avoid is changing the API unnecessarily.

If there's a way to implement the feature using existing APIs, we do it. This lets the back-end team focus on stability and performance by fixing bugs. They can't do that if the API constantly has to change in order to support our features.

Sometimes there's no getting around adding new back-end services. In order to scale our development process, we need to know when new services are necessary, and how to go about implementing them.

The first question is the necessity of the new service. Sometimes this is easy — it's not possible to implement the requested API. We'll have to make do with what's there. The second question is the feasibility of the new service. We'll likely form the shape of the new API since we're the ones who need it. Then we'll have to hear what the back-end team thinks. If we're a team with full-stack developers, there's less overhead because we're likely all on the same team and in closer communication with one another.

Now that we've decided to go ahead with the new API, we have to synchronize the implementation of our feature in the front-end, with the implementation of the feature in the back-end. There's no cut-and-dry solution here for us to follow, because the service could be easy or difficult to implement. Our feature could require several new services. The trick is reaching an agreement on the API and having a mocking mechanism in place. Once the real service is available, it's a time matter of disabling the mock.

However, in terms of scaling our application as a whole, this is just one integration point between the front-end features and back-end services. The implications of introducing the new feature, for the system, aren't known. We can only guess so much through testing and prior knowledge. It's not until production that we will see the full implication of how well our new feature scales. Different features that use the exact same service have different implications for request load, error rate, and so on.

Consuming real-time data

It's commonplace in JavaScript applications to have socketed connections to back-end data, in order to keep any user sessions synchronized with the reality. This simplifies some areas of our code while complicating others. The implications for scaling are substantial. Sending real-time data over web socket connections is what's called "pushing data". The prevailing technique prior to web socket connectivity was long-polling HTTP requests. This basically meant that instead of the data being delivered to clients when it changed, the client was responsible for checking if the data had changed.

The same scaling issues surrounding real-time data still exist today. With web socket technology, some of the burden has been shifted from our front-end code to the back-end. It's up to the application services to push web socket messages when relevant messages take place. There are a number of angles we need to look at here though. For example, does our architecture as a whole rely on the delivery of real-time data, or are we only considering real-time data for a single feature?

If we're considering introducing web-socket connectivity for the first time, to better support a new feature, we have to ask ourselves if it's something we want to fit into our architecture moving forward. The challenge with real-time data only affecting one or two features is a lack of clarity. Developers looking at one feature that has real-time data fed into it, versus another that does not, will have a hard time addressing things like consistency issues that arise over the course of developing our software.

It often makes more sense, and scales better from a number of perspectives, to properly integrate real-time data into the code of our front-end architecture. Which essentially means that any given component should have access to real-time data in the same way as any other component. As always though, the scaling issues we face when flowing top-down, from the user and their organization, ultimately determines the type of features we implement. This in turn influences the rate at which real-time data is published. Depending on the structure of our application, and how user data is connected, the frequency with which real-time data is delivered to each browser session can fluctuate dramatically. These types of considerations have to be made for every feature we implement.

Scaling features example

Our video conference software is popular with large organizations. Mainly due to it's stability, performance, and the fact that it's browser-based, without the need for plugins. One of our customers has requested that we implement chat utilities as well. They like our software so much that they'd rather use it for all real-time communication, and not just video conferencing.

The actual implementation of chat utilities at the JavaScript level wouldn't be too difficult. We would end up reusing several components that enable our web video conferencing functionality. A little re-factoring and we've got the new chat components that we need. But there're some subtle differences between text chat and video chat with regard to scale.

The key difference is the longevity of the text chats versus video chats, where the latter is generally a transient occurrence. This means that we need to figure out policies for persisting chats. Our video chats don't require user accounts to join, in case people want to invite people outside of the organization. This is different with text chats because we can't exactly invite anonymous actors, and then blow the chat away after they leave. We'll likely have other changes to make in our user management components as well. For example, do chat groups now correspond to video groups?

Since this is just one customer who's asked for this capability, we'll probably want a way to turn it off. Not only does this new feature have the potential to detract from our core value—video conferencing—but it can cause problems in deployments for other customers. With the new back-end services, the added interface complexity, and the additional training and support that's required, it's understandable that not all organizations would want this feature enabled. So if this isn't something we already have in our architecture, that is, the ability to turn components on and off, then that's something else that influences our ability to scale.

Scaling development

The last hurdle for us to overcome in terms of scaling influencers is that of actually developing the software. Any sufficiently complex JavaScript application isn't going to be written in isolation by just one developer. There's a team involved, even if it is only ad-hoc and self-organized in an open source context. In other institutions, teams and the roles within them are defined more concretely. Regardless of how the team is put together, scaling that team is a direct consequence of how we react to the other scaling influencers discussed so far in this chapter.

The first issue we'll address is the one we're most likely to run into first with a nascent software project—finding development resources. A team isn't a static thing; we'll have to add new resources as the software grows in code size and solution scope. Like it or not, the best resources are the most likely to leave as they're the most sought after. Ideally, we can hang on to a talented crew, but we will nonetheless have to scale the process of acquiring new resources. How and when we hire JavaScript programmers is influenced by the features we're implementing, and the architecture we're putting together to to serve the functioning of those features.

From a day-to-day perspective, each team member should be responsible for implementing a specific chunk of our application. This is a complicated matter, and scaling influencers are to blame. We have to be careful about defining our roles for the team; to not make them overly restrictive. When things change in response to influencers, we need to pivot and deliver. Rigid role definitions don't help us much here. Conversely, we need to at least make an attempt to put boundaries in place, if there's going to be any level of autonomy in the way our components are developed.

Finally, we'll try to figure out if there's a sound approach to determine when we potentially have too many development resources. To say it out loud almost sounds like a bad thing. We've got all this talent, and all this work to do—it seems like those two items go hand-in-hand, do they not? No, not always.

Finding development resources

It's tempting, especially for product managers, to hire development resources not for what we're currently working on, but for what we've planned to work on in the future. But this doesn't scale well for a number of reasons. The first issue that new hires are likely to face in this scenario is not being able to learn the code by working on real features. Remember, they were hired to work on something on the roadmap that we haven't started yet. So they end up trying to be useful, but there's no real obligation for them yet. After a couple of weeks, they're fighting to stay out of the way of folks who are trying to wrap up work.

It's often better to consider what we're working on now. Is there a clear gap in our ability to deliver something that's expected in the next release of our software? If there is no well-defined gap, there's nothing for a new programmer to fill, and that just creates unnecessary communication overhead. The downside is that once we have clearly-defined gaps in our ability to develop the features we need, we won't be able to find the resources we need. This pressure can lead to hiring the wrong people, who don't gel with the team, for one reason or another.

A better approach to scaling the growth of our development resources is to wait till there's a gap. A gap doesn't necessary mean the world is on fire and you're going to fail as a company. It just means we could do things better, development-wise. We shouldn't try hiring more than one developer at a time if we can avoid it. If we take the time needed to find the right resource, then they're likely to fill any gaps we've identified with our process and some.

The quintessential resource on communication overhead during the software development lifecycle is "The Mythical Man-Month", by Fred Brooks.

Development responsibilities

The web browser platform is a complex space, with lots of technologies, and lots of moving parts. Some components of the web platform are more greenfield than others, but important nonetheless for us to understand. These emerging technologies are the future of the web. So who on our team is going to take ownership of learning these new technologies and socializing them throughout the organization? The challenge with the web platform is that there's more to master than one person can reasonably manage while simultaneously delivering product features. This is why we need at least some level of development roles.

How strict the boundaries are for these roles is dependent on the organization and the culture therein. The nature of the application under development will likely influence the types of development roles to setup too. There's no recipe, and strictness should be avoided where possible. The reason being that we need to adapt to changes brought on by scaling influencers. Strict roles essentially impede an otherwise capable developer from putting out fires. We generally don't have time for role boundary disputes as deadlines loom.

It's the architect of the front-end that's most likely to see the roles that make sense for implementing a given application architecture. And these are likely transient roles, guided by the architect but formed organically by the members themselves. This is especially observable in open source projects where people do what they're good at, and hence what they enjoy doing. While we can't always adopt this model exactly, we can certainly take cues from it — shape roles around what people are good at doing in the context of our feature requirements. Doing so will help developers get mentorship where they need it. Being interested in some aspect of JavaScript development doesn't mean they're proficient at the level they need to be. That's where having a senior person show them the ropes, doing something they like doing, has enormous payoffs for the product in the long term.

Too many resources

We've partially addressed the notion that it's easy to hire too many development resources — tempting even. When there's a clear roadmap ahead of us defined by product management, we want to take comfort in knowing we do in fact have the development resources to fulfill our roadmap. Hiring people too fast inevitably leads to too many development resources. We may already be there now, and the question then becomes what to do about it.

If we're unhappy with members of our team, and it's clear that we have more resources than are needed, the answer is straightforward. However, there's another way to look at things, if we have too many good resources we don't want to lose. We have to adjust the product roadmap to accommodate the development talent we've recruited. This often means finding a channel in which we're able to flow product ideas up from development to product management. This is more of an art than a science.

It's a challenging job, being a front-end architect and figuring out who's going to build what. The best way to scale our development resources is to provide an accurate map of our architecture to those that are currently implementing it. If there's discrepancies, figure out the right path forward. For example, there could be gaps and we need more JavaScript programmers, or there could be too many resources and something needs to change in the product.

Scaling development example

Our application has been around for a while, has seen some success, and is deployed in a variety of contexts. One of our core developers, Ryan, touches many areas of the code. He helps many other developers improve their code, providing suggestions and so on. Our application has reached the point where it's large enough 'for us to start noticing performance degradation across all features.

We need Ryan to implement some performance enhancements, which will involve re-factoring certain sections of code, and basically occupy all his time. We still have features to deliver, if we plan on scaling to meet customer demand. On the other hand, we're seeing red flags with our ability to scale performance-wise.

We realize that we need to hire a new developer to help with new feature development. This developer doesn't need Ryan-like chops. They need to have the basics down for the technologies we're using. If we're lucky, we'll find someone that grows into filling more responsibilities. But for now, the gap left by Ryan that we need to fill is fairly narrow. And to scale, we don't need to find another Ryan right away.

Influencer checklist

We'll close out the chapter with a few checklists. These are simple questions for which there's no one correct answer. Some answers will remain the same throughout the lifetime of our software. For example, our business model will, hopefully, 'not change often. Others depend on the current state of things, and that's what these lists are for. We can come back to them again and again, anytime something changes. These could be requirements, users, new deployments, or changes to the development environment. These questions are nothing more than subtle reminders of the factors that influence scalable JavaScript applications. If reading them results in more questions than answers, then they've served their purpose.

User checklist

The user is why we build software in the first place. This checklist covers the most fundamental aspects of why we need to scale our application. These questions will be relevant throughout the lifetime of the software. And not just when something with the user management perspective is in question. Changes to feature development should trigger a look at this list.

What's the business model of our software?

- Is it *license-based*?
- Is it *subscription-based*?
- Is it *consumption-based*?
- Is it *advertisement-based*?
- Is it *open source*?

Does our application have different user roles?

- Are features hidden from one role while visible to others?
- Does every feature in our application have to be *role-aware*?
- How are roles defined and administered?
- How does our business model influence the use of roles in our application?

Do our users communicate with each other using our software?

- Do users collaborate with each other to use our application effectively?
- Does user communication happen as a side-effect of our data model?
- How do the user roles in our application influence user communication?

How do we support our application?

- Is support built into the application, or handled externally?
- Can users support each other using a central knowledge repository?
- How do our business model and application user roles influence the type of support we need to provide?

How do we collect feedback from users?

- Is feedback collection built into the application, or handled externally?
- How do we incentivize users to provide feedback?
- How does the type of support we provide influence the type of feedback we want to collect?

How do we notify users with relevant information?

- Does our application have a generic, context-independent notification mechanism?
- How do we ensure that only relevant notifications take place at any given time?
- Can users audit their notifications?

What type of user metrics should we collect?

- Do we use metrics to improve future versions of the product?
- Can our features use metrics at runtime to improve the user experience?
- How does the business model influence our need to collect metrics?

Feature checklist

Following the scaling influencers that originate from users of our software, are the features of our software. This list covers some of the questions we should be asking ourselves about any new feature, or implementing changes in an existing feature. They'll help us address the common issues related to scalability on a per-feature basis.

What's the core value proposition of our software?

- Does the feature we're implementing or enhancing contribute to the overall value proposition of our product?
- Is our current value proposition too broadly focused?
- How do the number of users and their roles influence our ability to focus on features relevant to our application's value?

How do we determine the feasibility of a feature?

- Are we trying to implement killer features instead of letting them come about naturally?
- Do we take the time to determine whether a proposed feature is feasible to implement, rather than implementing it poorly?
- How does the value proposition of our software, and the feature requests from our users, influence the feasibility of the features we ultimately implement?

Can we make informed decisions about our features?

- Do we have any user metric data on which we can base our decisions?
- Is there any historical data on similar features we've implemented in the past?
- How does our business model influence the data we can collect and use for decisions about the features of our application?

Who's our competition?

- Are we offering something similar to a competing product, done better?
- Are we in a niché market?
- What can we learn from competing products?
- How does our business model influence the amount of competition we face and the types of features we need to implement?

How do we make what we have better?

- Given the rate at which we're adding features, do we have enough time to maintain our existing features?
- Is it safe, architecturally, to modify a feature without breaking other features?
- How do our users influence the enhancements we make to existing features?
- How does our business model influence our ability to deploy product enhancements?

How do we integrate user management into our features?

- Are access control mechanisms generalized to the point that they're not a day-to-day concern for feature development?
- Can we organize our features into groups?
- Can users turn features on or off?
- How does the type of application we're building, in conjunction with our users and their roles, influence the complexity of our features?

Are our features tightly coupled to backend services?

- Are the existing services generic enough to handle the new feature we're implementing?
- Are we able to mock back-end services, running entirely in the browser?
- How do our features influence the design and capabilities of back-end services?

How does the frontend stay synchronized with backend data?

- Can we utilize web socket connectivity for push notifications?
- Does high user activity cause more messages to be delivered to other users?
- How does consuming real-time data influence the complexity of our features?

Developer checklist

The final checklist we'll want to review throughout the course of our software is concerned with development resources. This checklist won't be used as frequently as the users or the features lists. Nonetheless, it's important to make sure we're addressing the concerns that arise in terms of development resources.

How do we find the right development resources?

- Can we get by with the development resources we currently have?
- Do we need to revisit the features under development to accommodate the resources we have?
- Do we have the *right* development resources for the product we're building?

How do we allocate development responsibilities?

- How much overlap should there be between areas of responsibility?
- Do our current areas of responsibility reflect what we're building?
- How do the various skill-sets of our team members influence the responsibilities?

Can we avoid hiring too many resources?

- Are we hiring people too far in advance of actually needing them?

- Are we experiencing communication overhead due to too many resources?

- How does the number of features under development in parallel, influence the perception that more developers means more will be accomplished?

Summary

There are three main areas of concern when it comes to scaling influencers in JavaScript applications. Each area influences the area directly beneath it, until we ultimately hit the ground floor, where development takes place.

First and foremost are the users of our software. There are a number of user-related factors that influence the need for our software to scale. For instance, the business model our organization chooses subtly affects later decisions about our architecture. License-based deployments are likely to be deployed on-premise somewhere, and therefore more likely to require customizations. The combinations of complexities are endless, and they all stem from the users of our software.

The next major area we looked at were the features themselves. We have to take much of the insight gained from thinking about our users and their influence on scale, and provide this as input to our feature design. For example, a lot may happen in a short period of time, once people start using our software. How will this distract us from the core value of our application? Believe it or not, focus is something that needs to scale too.

Finally, there are the development activities. There's the team to build, and finding the right people isn't easy. Even if we have a team of solid developers in place, the responsibilities, and how they are influenced by the features and the people using them, needs to be taken into consideration. Likewise, as the development of our application progresses, we have to ensure that the right resources are in place.

Now that we've laid the foundation of what scaling is all about in the front-end, we're ready to dive into the specifics. The remainder of this book will put the concepts of the first two chapters into a JavaScript context. We know what scaling influencers are, and now we get to make architectural trade-offs. This is the fun part, because we get to write code.

3
Component Composition

Large-scale JavaScript applications amount to a series of communicating components. The focus of this chapter is on the composition of these components, while in the next chapter we will look at how these components communicate with one another. Composition is a big topic, and one that's relevant to scalable JavaScript code. When we start thinking about the composition of our components, we start to notice certain flaws in our design; limitations that prevent us from scaling in response to influencers.

The composition of a component isn't random — there's a handful of prevalent patterns for JavaScript components. We'll begin the chapter with a look at some of these generic component types that encapsulate common patterns found in every web application. Understanding that components implement patterns is crucial for extending these generic components in a way that scales.

It's one thing to get our component composition right from a purely technical standpoint, it's another to easily map these components to features. The same challenge holds true for components we've already implemented. The way we compose our code needs to provide a level of transparency, so that it's feasible to decompose our components and understand what they're doing, both at runtime and at design time.

Finally, we'll take a look at the idea of decoupling business logic from our components. This is nothing new — the idea of separation-of-concerns has been around for a long time. The challenge with JavaScript applications is that it touches on so many things — it's difficult to clearly separate business logic from other implementation concerns. The way in which we organize our source code (relative to the components that use them) can have a dramatic effect on our ability to scale.

Generic component types

It's exceedingly unlikely that anyone, in this day and age, would set out to build a large scale JavaScript application without the help of libraries, a framework, or both. Let's refer to these collectively as tools, since we're more interested in using the tools that help us scale, and not necessarily which tools are better than other tools. At the end of the day, it's up to the development team to decide which tool is best for the application we're building, personal preferences aside.

Guiding factors in choosing the tools we use are the type of components they provide, and what these are capable of. For example, a larger web framework may have all the generic components we need. On the other hand, a functional programming utility library might provide a lot of the low-level functionality we need. How these things are composed into a cohesive feature that scales, is for us to figure out.

The idea is to find tools that expose generic implementations of the components we need. Often, we'll extend these components, building specific functionality that's unique to our application. This section walks through the most typical components we'd want in a large-scale JavaScript application.

Modules

Modules exist, in one form or another, in almost every programming language. Except in JavaScript. That's almost untrue though—ECMAScript 6, in its final draft status at the time of this writing, introduces the notion of modules. However, there are tools out there today that allow us to modularize our code, without relying on the `script` tag. Large-scale JavaScript code is still a relatively new thing. Things such as the `script` tag weren't meant to address issues like modular code and dependency management.

RequireJS is probably the most popular module loader and dependency resolver. The fact that we need a library just to load modules into our front-end application speaks of the complexities involved. For example, module dependencies aren't a trivial matter when there's network latency and race conditions to consider.

Another option is to use a transpiler like **Browserify**. This approach is gaining traction because it lets us declare our modules using the CommonJS format. This format is used by NodeJS, and the upcoming ECMAScript module specification is a lot closer to CommonJS than to AMD. The advantage is that the code we write today has better compatibility with back-end JavaScript code, and with the future.

Some frameworks, such as Angular or Marionette, have their own ideas of what modules are- albeit, more abstract ideas.

These modules are more about organizing our code, than they are about tactfully delivering code from the server to the browser. These types of modules might even map better to other features of the framework. For example, if there's a centralized application instance that's used to manage our modules, the framework might provide a mean to manage modules from the application. Take a look at the following diagram:

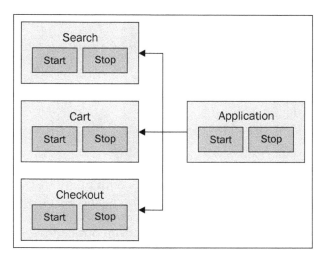

A global application component using modules as it's building blocks. Modules can be small, containing only one feature, or large, containing several features

This lets us perform higher-level tasks at the module level (things such as disabling modules or configuring them with arguments). Essentially, modules speak for features. They're a packaging mechanism that allow us to encapsulate things about a given feature that the rest of the application doesn't care about. Modules help us scale our application by adding high-level operations to our features, by treating our features as the building blocks. Without modules, we'd have no meaningful way to do this.

The composition of modules look different depending on the mechanism used to declare the module. A module could be straightforward, providing a namespace from which objects can be exported. Or if we're using a specific framework module flavor, there could be much more to it. Like automatic event life cycles, or methods for performing **boilerplate** setup tasks.

However we slice it, modules in the context of scalable JavaScript are a means to create larger building blocks, and a means to handling complex dependencies:

```
// main.js
// Imports a log() function from the util.js model.
import log from 'util.js';
log('Initializing...');

// util.js
// Exports a basic console.log() wrapper function.
'use strict';

export default function log(message) {
    if (console) {
        console.log(message);
    }
}
```

While it's easier to build large-scale applications with module-sized building blocks, it's also easier to tear a module out of an application and work with it in isolation. If our application is monolithic or our modules are too plentiful and fine-grained, it's very difficult for us to excise problem-spots from our code, or to test work in progress. Our component may function perfectly well on its own. It could have negative side-effects somewhere else in the system, however. If we can remove pieces of the puzzle, one at a time and without too much effort, we can scale the trouble-shooting process.

Routers

Any large-scale JavaScript application has a significant number of possible URIs. The URI is the address of the page that the user is looking at. They can navigate to this resource by clicking links, or they may be taken to a new URI automatically by our code, perhaps in response to some user action. The web has always relied on URIs, long before the advent of large-scale JavaScript applications. URIs point to resources, and resources can be just about anything. The larger the application, the more resources, and the more potential URIs.

Router components are tools that we use in the front-end, to listen for these URI change events and respond to them accordingly. There's less reliance on the back-end web servers parsing the URI, and returning the new content. Most web sites still do this, but there are several disadvantages with this approach when it comes to building applications:

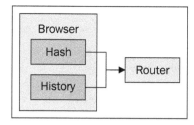

The browser triggers events when the URI changes, and the router component responds to these changes. The URI changes can be triggered from the history API, or from `location.hash`

The main problem is that we want the UI to be portable, as in, we want to be able to deploy it against any back-end and things should work. Since we're not assembling markup for the URI in the back-end, it doesn't make sense to parse the URI in the back-end either.

We declaratively specify all the URI patterns in our router components. We generally refer to these as, **routes**. Think of a route as a blueprint, and a URI as an instance of that blueprint. This means that when the router receives a URI, it can correlate it to a route. That, in essence, is the responsibility of router components. Which is easy with smaller applications, but when we're talking about scale, further deliberation on router design is in order.

As a starting point, we have to consider the URI mechanism we want to use. The two choices are basically listening to hash change events, or utilizing the history API. Using hash-bang URIs is probably the simplest approach. The `history` API available in every modern browser, on the other hand, lets us format URI's without the hash-bang—they look like real URIs. The router component in the framework we're using may support only one or the other, thus simplifying the decision. Some support both URI approaches, in which case we need to decide which one works best for our application.

The next thing to consider about routing in our architecture is how to react to route changes. There are generally two approaches to this. The first is to declaratively bind a route to a callback function. This is ideal when the router doesn't have a lot of routes. The second approach is to trigger events when routes are activated. This means that there's nothing directly bound to the router. Instead, some other component listens for such an event. This approach is beneficial when there are lots of routes, because the router has no knowledge of the components, just the routes.

Here's an example that shows a router component listening to route events:

```js
// router.js

import Events from 'events.js'

// A router is a type of event broker, it
// can trigger routes, and listen to route
// changes.
export default class Router extends Events {

    // If a route configuration object is passed,
    // then we iterate over it, calling listen()
    // on each route name. This is translating from
    // route specs to event listeners.
    constructor(routes) {
        super();

        if (routes != null) {
            for (let key of Object.keys(routes)) {
                this.listen(key, routes[key]);
            }
        }
    }

    // This is called when the caller is ready to start
    // responding to route events. We listen to the
    // "onhashchange" window event. We manually call
    // our handler here to process the current route.
    start() {
        window.addEventListener('hashchange',
            this.onHashChange.bind(this));

        this.onHashChange();
    }

    // When there's a route change, we translate this into
    // a triggered event. Remember, this router is also an
    // event broker. The event name is the current URI.
    onHashChange() {
        this.trigger(location.hash, location.hash);
    }

};
```

```
// Creates a router instance, and uses two different
// approaches to listening to routes.
//
// The first is by passing configuration to the Router.
// The key is the actual route, and the value is the
// callback function.
//
// The second uses the listen() method of the router,
// where the event name is the actual route, and the
// callback function is called when the route is activated.
//
// Nothing is triggered until the start() method is called,
// which gives us an opportunity to set everything up. For
// example, the callback functions that respond to routes
// might require something to be configured before they can
// run.

import Router from 'router.js'

function logRoute(route) {
    console.log('${route} activated');
}

var router = new Router({
    '#route1': logRoute
});

router.listen('#route2', logRoute);

router.start();
```

Some of the code required to run these examples is omitted from the listings. For example, the events.js module is included in the code bundle that comes with this book, it's just not that relevant to the example.

Also in the interest of space, the code examples avoid using specific frameworks and libraries. In practice, we're not going to write our own router or events API—our frameworks do that already. We're instead using vanillaES6 JavaScript, to illustrate points pertinent to scaling our applications.

Another architectural consideration we'll want to make when it comes to routing is whether we want a global, monolithic router, a router per module, or some other component. The downside to having a monolithic router is that it becomes difficult to scale when it grows sufficiently large, as we keep adding features and routes. The advantage is that the routes are all declared in one place. Monolithic routers can still trigger events that all our components can listen to.

The per-module approach to routing involves multiple router instances. For example, if our application has five components, each would have their own router. The advantage here is that the module is completely self-contained. Anyone working with this module doesn't need to look elsewhere to figure out which routes it responds to. Using this approach, we can also have a tighter coupling between the route definitions and the functions that respond to them, which could mean simpler code. The downside to this approach is that we lose the consolidated aspect of having all our routes declared in a central place. Take a look at the following diagram:

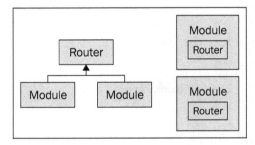

The router to the left is global—all modules use the same instance to respond to URI events. The modules to the right have their own routers. These instances contain configuration specific to the module, not the entire application

Depending on the capabilities of the framework we're using, the router components may or may not support multiple router instances. It may only be possible to have one callback function per route. There may be subtle nuances to the router events we're not yet aware of.

Models/Collections

The API our application interacts with exposes entities. Once these entities have been transferred to the browser, we will store a model of those entities. Collections are a bunch of related entities, usually of the same type.

The tools we're using may or may not provide a generic model and/or collection components, or they may have something similar but named differently. The goal of modeling API data is a rough approximation of the API entity. This could be as simple as storing models as plain JavaScript objects and collections as arrays.

The challenge with simply storing our API entities as plain objects in arrays is that some other component is then responsible for talking to the API, triggering events when the data changes, and for performing data transformations. We want other components to be able to transform collections and models where needed, in order to fulfill their duties. But we don't want repetitive code, and it's best if we're able to encapsulate the common things like transformations, API calls, and event life cycles. Take a look at the next diagram:

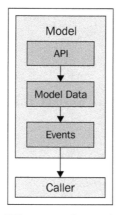

Models encapsulate interaction with APIs, parsing data, and triggering events when data changes.
This leads to simpler code outside of the models

Hiding the details of how the API data is loaded into the browser, or how we issue commands, helps us scale our application as we grow. As we add more entities to the API, the complexity of our code grows too. We can throttle this complexity by constraining the API interactions to our model and collection components.

Downloading the example code

You can download the example code files from your account at http://www.packtpub.com for all the Packt Publishing books you have purchased. If you purchased this book elsewhere, you can visit http://www.packtpub.com/support and register to have the files e-mailed directly to you.

Another scalability issue we'll face with our models and collections is where they fit in the big picture. That is, our application is really just one big component, composed of smaller components. Our models and collections map well to our API, but not necessarily to features. API entities are more generic than specific features, and are often used by several features. Which leaves us with an open question—where do our models and collections fit into components?

Here's an example that shows specific views extending generic views. The same model can be passed to both:

```
// A super simple model class.
class Model {
    constructor(first, last, age) {
        this.first = first;
        this.last = last;
        this.age = age;
    }
}


// The base view, with a name method that
// generates some output.
class BaseView {
    name() {
        return '${this.model.first} ${this.model.last}';
    }
}


// Extends BaseView with a constructor that accepts
// a model and stores a reference to it.
class GenericModelView extends BaseView {
    constructor(model) {
        super();
        this.model = model;
    }
}


// Extends GenericModelView with specific constructor
// arguments.
class SpecificModelView extends BaseView {
    constructor(first, last, age) {
        super();
        this.model = new Model(...arguments);
    }
}
```

```
var properties = [ 'Terri', 'Hodges', 41 ];

// Make sure the data is the same in both views.
// The name() method should return the same result...
console.log('generic view',
    new GenericModelView(new Model(...properties)).name());
console.log('specific view',
    new SpecificModelView(...properties).name());
```

On one hand, components can be completely generic with regard to the models and collections they use. On the other hand, some components are specific with their requirements—they can directly instantiate their collections. Configuring generic components with specific models and collections at runtime only benefits us when the component truly is generic, and is used in several places. Otherwise, we might as well encapsulate the models within the components that use them. Choosing the right approach helps us scale. Because, not all our components will be entirely generic or entirely specific.

Controllers/Views

Depending on the framework we're using, and the design patterns our team is following, controllers and views can represent different things. There's simply too many MV* pattern and style variations to provide a meaningful distinction in terms of scale. The minute differences have trade-offs relative to similar but different MV* approaches. For our purpose of discussing large scale JavaScript code, we'll treat them as the same type of component. If we decide to separate the two concepts in our implementation, the ideas in this section will be relevant to both types.

Let's stick with the term views for now, knowing that we're covering both views and controllers, conceptually. These components interact with several other component types, including routers, models or collections, and templates, which are discussed in the next section. When something happens, the user needs to be notified about it. The view's job is to update the DOM.

This could be as simple as changing an attribute on a DOM element, or as involved as rendering a new template:

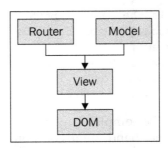

A view component updating the DOM in response to router and model events

A view can update the DOM in response to several types of events. A route could have changed. A model could have been updated. Or something more direct, like a method call on the view component. Updating the DOM is not as straightforward as one might think. There's the performance to think about—what happens when our view is flooded with events? There's the latency to think about—how long will this JavaScript call stack run, before stopping and actually allowing the DOM to render?

Another responsibility of our views is responding to DOM events. These are usually triggered by the user interacting with our UI. The interaction may start and end with our view. For example, depending on the state of something like user input or one of our models, we might update the DOM with a message. Or we might do nothing, if the event handler is **debounced**, for instance.

A debounced function groups multiple calls into one. For example, calling foo() 20 times in 10 milliseconds may only result in the implementation of foo() being called once. For a more detailed explanation, look at: http://drupalmotion.com/article/debounce-and-throttle-visual-explanation. Most of the time, the DOM events get translated into something else, either a method call or another event. For example, we might call a method on a model, or transform a collection. The end result, most of the time, is that we provide feedback by updating the DOM.

This can be done either directly, or indirectly. In the case of direct DOM updates, it's simple to scale. In the case of indirect updates, or updates through side-effects, scaling becomes more of a challenge. This is because as the application acquires more moving parts, the more difficult it becomes to form a mental map of cause and effect.

Here's an example that shows a view listening to DOM events and model events.

```
import Events from 'events.js';

// A basic model. It extending "Events" so it
// can listen to events triggered by other components.
class Model extends Events {
    constructor(enabled) {
        super();
        this.enabled = !!enabled;
    }

    // Setters and getters for the "enabled" property.
    // Setting it also triggers an event. So other components
    // can listen to the "enabled" event.
    set enabled(enabled) {
        this._enabled = enabled;
        this.trigger('enabled', enabled);
    }

    get enabled() {
        return this._enabled;
    }
}

// A view component that takes a model and a DOM element
// as arguments.
class View {
    constructor(element, model) {

        // When the model triggers the "enabled" event,
        // we adjust the DOM.
        model.listen('enabled', (enabled) => {
            element.setAttribute('disabled', !enabled);
        });

        // Set the state of the model when the element is
        // clicked. This will trigger the listener above.
        element.addEventListener('click', () => {
            model.enabled = false;
```

```
        });
    }
}

new View(document.getElementById('set'), new Model());
```

On the plus side to all this complexity, we actually get some reusable code. The view is agnostic as to how the model or router it's listening to is updated. All it cares about is specific events on specific components. This is actually helpful to us because it reduces the amount of special-case handling we need to implement.

The DOM structure that's generated at runtime, as a result of rendering all our views, needs to be taken into consideration as well. For example, if we look at some of the top-level DOM nodes, they have nested structure within them. It's these top-level nodes that form the skeleton of our layout. Perhaps this is rendered by the main application view, and each of our views has a child-relationship to it. Or perhaps the hierarchy extends further down than that. The tools we're using most likely have mechanisms for dealing with these parent-child relationships. However, bear in mind that vast view hierarchies are difficult to scale.

Templates

Template engines used to reside mostly in the back-end framework. That's less true today, thanks largely to the sophisticated template rendering libraries available in the front-end. With large-scale JavaScript applications, we rarely talk to back-end services about UI-specific things. We don't say, "here's a URL, render the HTML for me". The trend is to give our JavaScript components a certain level autonomy — letting them render their own markup.

Having component markup coupled with the components that render them is a good thing. It means that we can easily discern where the markup in the DOM is being generated. We can then diagnose issues and tweak the design of a large scale application.

Templates help establish a separation of concerns with each of our components. The markup that's rendered in the browser mostly comes from the template. This keeps markup-specific code out of our JavaScript. Front-end template engines aren't just tools for string replacement; they often have other tools to help reduce the amount of boilerplate JavaScript code to write. For example, we can embed things like conditionals and for-each loops in our markup, where they're suited.

Application-specific components

The component types we've discussed so far are very useful for implementing scalable JavaScript code, but they're also very generic. Inevitably, during implementation we're going to hit a road block—the component composition patterns we've been following will not work for certain features. This is when it's time to step back and think about possibly adding a new type of component to our architecture.

For example, consider the idea of widgets. These are generic components that are mainly focused on presentation and user interactions. Let's say that many of our views are using the exact same DOM elements, and the exact same event handlers. There's no point in repeating them in every view throughout our application. Might it not be better if we were to factor it into a common component? A view might be overkill, so perhaps we need a new type of widget component?

Sometimes we'll create components for the sole purpose of composition. For example, we might have a component that glues together router, view, model/collection, and template components together to form a cohesive unit. Modules partially solve this problem but they aren't always enough. Sometimes we're missing that added bit of orchestration that our components need in order to communicate. We'll cover communicating components in the next chapter.

Extending generic components

We often discover, late in the development process, that the components we rely on are lacking something we need. If the base component we're using is designed well, then we can extend it, plugging in the new properties or functionality we need. In this section, we'll walk through some scenarios where we might need to extend the common generic components used throughout our application.

If we're going to scale our code, we need to leverage these base components where we can. We'll probably want to start extending our own base components at some point too. Some tools are better than others at facilitating the extension mechanism through which we implement this specialized behavior.

Identifying common data and functionality

Before we look at extending the specific component types, it's worthwhile to consider the common properties and functionality that's common across all component types. Some of these things will be obvious up-front, while others are less pronounced. Our ability to scale depends, in part, on our ability to identify commonality across our components.

If we have a global application instance, quite common in large JavaScript applications, global values and functionality can live there. This can grow unruly down the line though, as more common things are discovered. Another approach might be to have several global modules, instead of just a single application instance. Or both. But this doesn't scale from an understandability perspective:

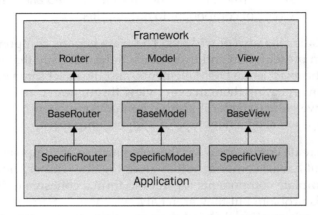

The ideal component hierarchy doesn't extend beyond three levels. The top level is usually found in a framework our application depends on

As a rule-of-thumb, we should, for any given component, avoid extending it more than three levels down. For example, a generic view component from the tools we're using could be extended by our generic version of it. This would include properties and functionality that every view instance in our application requires. This is only a two-level hierarchy, and easy to manage. This means that if any given component needs to extend our generic view, it can do so without complicating things. Three-levels should be the maximum extension hierarchy depth for any given type. This is just enough to avoid unnecessary global data, going beyond this presents scaling issues because the hierarchy isn't easily grasped.

Extending router components

Our application may only require a single router instance. Even in this case, we may still need to override certain extension points of the generic router. In case of multiple router instances, there's bound to be common properties and functionality that we don't want to repeat. For example, if every route in our application follows the same pattern, with only subtle differences, we can implement the tools in our base router to avoid repetitious code.

In addition to declaring routes, events take place when a given route is activated. Depending on the architecture of our application, different things need to happen. Maybe certain things always need to happen, no matter which route has been activated. This is where extending the router to provide our own functionality comes in handy. For example, we have to validate permission for a given route. It wouldn't make much sense for us to handle this through individual components, as this would not scale well with complex access control rules and a lot of routes.

Extending models/collections

Our models and collections, no matter what their specific implementation look like, will share some common properties with one another- especially if they're targeting the same API, which is the common case. The specifics of a given model or collection revolve around the API endpoint, the data returned, and the possible actions taken. It's likely that we'll target the same base API path for all entities, and that all entities have a handful of shared properties. Rather than repeat ourselves in every model or collection instance, it's better to abstract the common data.

In addition to sharing properties among our models and collections, we can share common behavior. For instance, it's quite likely that a given model isn't going to have sufficient data for a given feature. Perhaps that data can be derived by transforming the model. These types of transformations can be common, and abstracted in a base model or collection. It really depends on the types of features we're implementing and how consistent they are with one another. If we're growing fast and getting lots of requests for "outside-the-box" features, then we're more likely to implement data transformations inside the views that require these one-off changes to the models or collections they're using.

Most frameworks take care of the nuances for performing XHR requests to fetch our data or perform actions. That's not the whole story unfortunately, because our features will rarely map one-to-one with a single API entity. More likely, we will have a feature that requires several collections that are related to one another somehow, and a transformed collection. This type of operation can grow complex quickly, because we have to work with multiple XHR requests.

We'll likely use promises to synchronize the fetching of these requests, and then perform the data transformation once we have all the necessary sources.

Here's an example that shows a specific model extending a generic model, to provide new fetching behavior:

```
// The base fetch() implementation of a model, sets
// some property values, and resolves the promise.
class BaseModel {
    fetch() {
        return new Promise((resolve, reject) => {
            this.id = 1;
            this.name = 'foo';
            resolve(this);
        });
    }
}


// Extends BaseModel with a specific implementation
// of fetch().
class SpecificModel extends BaseModel {

    // Overrides the base fetch() method. Returns
    // a promise with combines the original
    // implementation and result of calling fetchSettings().
    fetch() {
        return Promise.all([
            super.fetch(),
            this.fetchSettings()
        ]);
    }

    // Returns a new Promise instance. Also sets a new
    // model property.
    fetchSettings() {
        return new Promise((resolve, reject) => {
            this.enabled = true;
            resolve(this);
        });
    }
}
```

```
// Make sure the properties are all in place, as expected,
// after the fetch() call completes.
new SpecificModel().fetch().then((result) => {
    var [ model ] = result;
    console.assert(model.id === 1, 'id');
    console.assert(model.name === 'foo');
    console.assert(model.enabled, 'enabled');
    console.log('fetched');
});
```

Extending controllers/views

When we have a base model or base collection, there are often properties shared between our controllers or views. That's because the job of a controller or a view is to render model or collection data. For example, if the same view is rendering the same model properties over and over, we can probably move that bit to a base view, and extend from that. Perhaps the repetitive parts are in the templates themselves. This means that we might want to consider having a base template inside a base view, as shown in the following diagram. Views that extend this base view, inherit this base template.

Depending on the library or framework at our disposal, extending templates in this way may not be feasible. Or the nature of our features may make this difficult to achieve. For example, there may not be a common base template, but there might be a lot of smaller views and templates that can plug-into larger components:

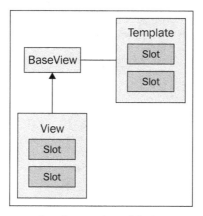

A view that extends a base view can populate the template of the base view, as well as inherit other base view functionalities

Our views also need to respond to user interactions. They may respond directly, or forward the events up the component hierarchy. In either case, if our features are at all consistent, there will be some common DOM event handling that we'll want to abstract into a common base view. This is a huge help in scaling our application, because as we add more features, the DOM event handling code additions is minimized.

Mapping features to components

Now that we have a handle on the most common JavaScript components, and the ways we'll want to extend them for use in our application, it's time to think about how to glue those components together. A router on it's own isn't very useful. Nor is a standalone model, template, or controller. Instead, we want these things to work together, to form a cohesive unit that realizes a feature in our application.

To do that, we have to map our features to components. We can't do this haphazardly either—we need to think about what's generic about our feature, and about what makes it unique. These feature properties will guide our design decisions on producing something that scales.

Generic features

Perhaps the most important aspects of component composition are consistency and reusability. While considering the scaling influences our application faces, we'll come up with a list of traits that all our components must carry: things such as user management, access control, and other traits unique to our application. This is along with the other architectural perspectives (explored in more depth throughout the remainder of the book), which form the core of our generic features:

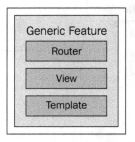

A generic component, composed of other generic components from our framework

The generic aspects of every feature in our application serve as a blueprint. They inform us in composing larger building blocks. These generic features account for the architectural factors that help us scale. And if we can encode these factors as parts of an aggregate component, we'll have an easier time scaling our application.

What makes this design task challenging is that we have to look at these generic components not only from a scalable architecture perspective, but also from a feature-complete perspective. If every feature behaved the same way, we'd be all set. If only every feature followed an identical pattern, the sky's the limit when it comes time to scale.

But 100% consistent feature functionality is an illusion, more visible to JavaScript programmers than to users. The pattern breaks out of necessity. It's responding to this breakage in a scalable way that matters. This is why successful JavaScript applications will continuously revisit the generic aspects of our features to ensure they reflect reality.

Specific features

When it's time to implement something that doesn't fit the pattern, we're faced with a scaling challenge. We have to pivot, and consider the consequences of introducing such a feature into our architecture. When patterns are broken, our architecture needs to change. This isn't a bad thing—it's a necessity. The limiting factor in our ability to scale in response to these new features, lies with generic aspects of our existing features. This means that we can't be too rigid with our generic feature components. If we're too demanding, we're setting ourselves up for failure.

Before making any brash architectural decisions stemming from offbeat features, think about the specific scaling consequences. For example, does it really matter that the new feature uses a different layout and requires a template that's different from all other feature components? The state of the JavaScript scaling art revolves around finding the handful of essential blueprints to follow for our component composition. Everything else is up for discussion on how to proceed.

Decomposing components

Component composition is an activity that creates order; larger behavior out of smaller parts. We often need to move in the opposite direction during development. Even after development, we can learn how a component works by tearing the code apart and watching it run in different contexts. Component decomposition means that we're able to take the system apart and examine individual parts in a somewhat structured approach.

Maintaining and debugging components

Over the course of application development, our components accumulate abstractions. We do this to support a feature's requirement better, while simultaneously supporting some architectural property that helps us scale. The problem is that as the abstractions accumulate, we lose transparency into the functioning of our components. This is not only essential for diagnosing and fixing issues, but also in terms of how easy the code is to learn.

For example, if there's a lot of indirection, it takes longer for a programmer to trace cause to effect. Time wasted on tracing code, reduces our ability to scale from a developmental point of view. We're faced with two opposing problems. First, we need abstractions to address real world feature requirements and architectural constraints. Second, is our inability to master our own code due to a lack of transparency.

Following is an example that shows a renderer component and a feature component. Renderers used by the feature are easily substitutable:

```
// A Renderer instance takes a renderer function
// as an argument. The render() method returns the
// result of calling the function.
class Renderer {
    constructor(renderer) {
        this.renderer = renderer;
    }

    render() {
        return this.renderer ? this.renderer(this) : '';
    }
}

// A feature defines an output pattern. It accepts
// header, content, and footer arguments. These are
// Renderer instances.
class Feature {
    constructor(header, content, footer) {
        this.header = header;
        this.content = content;
        this.footer = footer;
    }

    // Renders the sections of the view. Each section
    // either has a renderer, or it doesn't. Either way,
    // content is returned.
    render() {
```

```
        var header = this.header ?
            '${this.header.render()}\n' : '',
        content = this.content ?
            '${this.content.render()}\n' : '',
        footer = this.footer ?
            this.footer.render() : '';

        return '${header}${content}${footer}';
    }
}

// Constructs a new feature with renderers for three sections.
var feature = new Feature(
    new Renderer(() => { return 'Header'; }),
    new Renderer(() => { return 'Content'; }),
    new Renderer(() => { return 'Footer'; })
);

console.log(feature.render());

// Remove the header section completely, replace the footer
// section with a new renderer, and check the result.
delete feature.header;
feature.footer = new Renderer(() => { return 'Test Footer'; });

console.log(feature.render());
```

A tactic that can help us cope with these two opposing scaling influencers is substitutability. In particular, the ease with which one of our components, or sub-components, can be replaced with something else. This should be really easy to do. So before we go introducing layers of abstraction, we need to consider how easy it's going to be to replace a complex component with a simple one. This can help programmers learn the code, and also help with debugging.

For example, if we're able to take a complex component out of the system and replace it with a dummy component, we can simplify the debugging process. If the error goes away after the component is replaced, we have found the problematic component. Otherwise, we can rule out a component and keep digging elsewhere.

Re-factoring complex components

It's of course easier said than done to implement substitutability with our components, especially in the face of deadlines. Once it becomes impractical to easily replace components with others, it's time to consider re-factoring our code. Or at least the parts that make substitutability infeasible. It's a balancing act, getting the right level of encapsulation, and the right level of transparency.

Substitution can also be helpful at a more granular level. For example, let's say a view method is long and complex. If there are several stages during the execution of that method, where we would like to run something custom, we can't. It's better to re-factor the single method into a handful of methods, each of which can be overridden.

Pluggable business logic

Not all of our business logic needs to live inside our components, encapsulated from the outside world. Instead, it would be ideal if we could write our business logic as a set of functions. In theory, this provides us with a clear separation of concerns. The components are there to deal with the specific architectural concerns that help us scale, and the business logic can be plugged into any component. In practice, excising business logic from components isn't trivial.

Extending versus configuring

There are two approaches we can take when it comes to building our components. As a starting point, we have the tools provided by our libraries and frameworks. From there, we can keep extending these tools, getting more specific as we drill deeper and deeper into our features. Alternatively, we can provide our component instances with configuration values. These instruct the component on how to behave.

The advantage of extending things that would otherwise need to be configured is that the caller doesn't need to worry about them. And if we can get by, using this approach, all the better, because it leads to simpler code- especially the code that's using the component. On the other hand, we could have generic feature components that can be used for a specific purpose, if only they support this configuration or that configuration option. This approach has the advantage of using simpler component hierarchies, and less overall components.

Sometimes it's better to keep components as generic as possible, within the realm of understandability. That way, when we need a generic component for a specific feature, we can use it without having to re-define our hierarchy. Of course, there's more complexity involved for the caller of that component, because they need to supply it with the configuration values.

This is all a trade-off that's up to us, the JavaScript architects of our application. Do we want to encapsulate everything, configure everything, or do we want to strike a balance between the two?

Stateless business logic

With functional programming, functions don't have side effects. In some languages, this property is enforced, in JavaScript it isn't. However, we can still implement side-effect-free functions in JavaScript. If a function takes arguments, and always returns the same output based on those arguments, then the function can be said to be stateless. It doesn't depend on the state of a component, and it doesn't change the state of a component. It just computes a value.

If we can establish a library of business logic that's implemented this way, we can design some super flexible components. Rather than implement this logic directly in a component, we pass the behavior into the component. That way, different components can utilize the same stateless business logic functions.

The tricky part is finding the right functions that can be implemented this way as it's not a good idea to implement these up-front. Instead, as the iterations of our application development progress, we can use this strategy to re-factor code into generic stateless functions that are shared by any component capable of using them. This leads to business logic that's implemented in a focused way, and components that are small, generic, and reusable in a variety of contexts.

Organizing component code

In addition to composing our components in such a way that helps our application scale, we need to consider the structure of our source code modules too. When we first start off with a given project, our source code files tend to map well to what's running in the client's browser. Over time, as we accumulate more features and components, earlier decisions on how to organize our source tree can dilute this strong mapping.

When tracing runtime behavior to our source code, the less mental effort involved, the better. We can scale to more stable features this way because our efforts are focused more on the design problems of the day—the things that directly provide customer value:

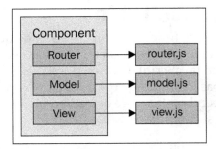

The diagram shows the mapping component parts to their implementation artifacts

There's another dimension to code organization in the context of our architecture, and that's our ability to isolate specific code. We should treat our code just like our runtime components, which are self-sustained units that we can turn on or off. That is, we should be able to find all the source code files required for a given component, without having to hunt them down. If a component requires, say, 10 source code files—JavaScript, HTML, and CSS—then ideally these should all be found in the same directory.

The exception, of course, is generic base functionality that's shared by all components. These should be as close to the surface as possible, then it's easy to trace our component dependencies; they all point to the top of the hierarchy. It's a challenge to scale the dependency graph when our component dependencies are all over the place.

Summary

This chapter introduced us to the concept of component composition. Components are the building blocks of a scalable JavaScript application. The common components we're likely to encounter include things like modules, models/collections, controllers/views, and templates. While these patterns help us achieve a level of consistency, they're not enough on their own to make our code work well under various scaling influencers. This is why we need to extend these components, providing our own generic implementations that specific features of our application can further extend and use.

Depending on the various scaling factors our application encounters, different approaches may be taken in getting generic functionality into our components. One approach is to keep extending the component hierarchy, and keep everything encapsulated and hidden away from the outside world. Another approach is to plug logic and properties into components when they're created. The cost is more complexity for the code that's using the components.

We ended the chapter with a look at how we might go about organizing our source code; so that it's structure better reflects that of our logical component design. This helps us scale our development effort, and helps isolate one component's code from others'. In the next chapter, we'll look in more detail at the space in between our components. It's one thing to have well crafted components that stand by themselves. It's quite another to implement scalable component communication.

4
Component Communication and Responsibilities

The preceding chapter focused on the *what* of components — what are they composed of and *why*. This chapter focuses on the glue in between our JavaScript components — the *how*. If our components are designed with a particular purpose in mind, then they need to communicate with other components to realize larger behavior. For example, a router component is unlikely to update the DOM or talk to the API. We have components that are good at those tasks, so other components can ask them to perform them, by communicating with them.

We'll start the chapter off with a look at communication models prevalent in frontend development. It's highly unlikely that we'll develop our own framework for inter-component communication since there are lots of robust libraries that already do this. What we're more interested in, from a JavaScript scaling perspective, is how the chosen communication model in our application prevents us from scaling, and what can be done about it.

The responsibilities of a given component influence how it communicates with our own components, as well as services beyond our control, like backend APIs and DOM APIs. Once we start implementing the components of our application, layers start to reveal themselves, and if stated explicitly, these are useful for visualizing communication flows. This allows us to anticipate future component communication scaling issues.

Communication models

There are various communication models we can use to enable inter-component communication. The simplest would be method invocations, or function calls. This approach is the most direct and the easiest to implement. However, there's also a deep coupling between one component that directly invokes method of another. This can't scale beyond a couple components.

Instead, we need a level of indirection between our components; something that mediates the communication from one component to another. This helps us to scale our inter-component communication because we're no longer communicating directly with other components. Instead, we're relying on our communication mechanism to fulfill message delivery. The two prevalent models for such a communication mechanism are message passing and event triggering. Let's compare the two approaches.

Message-passing models

Message-passing communication models are commonplace in JavaScript applications. For example, messages can be passed from one process to another on a local machine; they can be passed from one host to another, or they can be passed around in the same process. Although message-passing is somewhat abstract, it's still a fairly low-level idea—there's much room for interpretation. It's the mechanism that sits in between two communicating components that provide high-level abstractions.

For example, **publish-subscribe** is a more specific type of message-passing communication model. The mechanism that fulfills these messages is usually called a broker. A component will subscribe to messages of a particular topic, while other components will publish messages on that topic. The key design feature is that the components are unaware of one another. This promotes loose coupling between components, and helps us scale when there are lots of components.

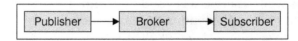

This shows a publish-subscribe model, using a broker to deliver published messages to subscribers

Another type of message passing abstraction is **command-response**. Here, one component issues a command to another component and gets a response. The coupling in this scenario is a little tighter, because the caller is targeting a specific component to fulfill the command.

However, this is still preferred over direct command invocation because we can still substitute both the caller and the receiver easily.

Event models

We often hear that user interface code is event-driven, that is, some event takes place, causing the UI to re-render a section. Or, the user performs some action in the UI, triggering an event that our code must interpret and act upon. From a communication perspective, UIs are just a bunch of declarative visual elements; events that are triggered, and the callback functions that respond to those events.

This is why the publish-subscribe model fits well with UI development. Most components we develop will trigger one or more event types, while other components will subscribe to this type of event and run code in response to it's triggering. This, at a high level, is how most of our components will communicate with one another—through events, which is really just publish-subscribe.

Speaking in terms of events and triggering, instead of messages and publish-subscribe, makes sense because it's the more familiar terminology with JavaScript developers. For example, there's the DOM and it's whole event system found there. They are the asynchronous events associated with Ajax calls and `Promise` objects, then there's the homegrown event system used by the framework our application leverages.

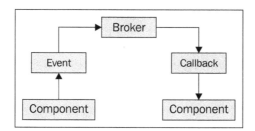

Events are triggered by one component while another component listening for that event executes a callback; this process is orchestrated by an event-broker mechanism

Needless to say, separate event systems that all trigger events through our application components make it difficult to mentally grasp what's actually happening in response to a given action. This is indeed a scaling problem, and the various sections throughout this chapter will dig into solutions that enable us to scale our component communication.

Communication data schema

Event data isn't opaque—it has meaning that our callback functions use to make decisions on how to react. Sometimes, this data is unneeded and can be safely ignored by the callback function. However, we don't want to decide, early on, that some callback added later on isn't going to need this data. And that's something that helps our communication mechanism scale—providing the right data in the right place.

Not only does the data need to be there, readily available for consumption by each callback function, but it also needs to have a predictable structure. We'll look at approaches to establish naming conventions for the event names themselves, as well as the data that's passed along to the handler functions. We can make inter-component communication a little more transparent, and thus more scalable, by making sure that the required event data is present and unlikely to be misinterpreted.

Naming conventions

Coming up with meaningful names is hard, especially when there are a lot of things to name, as is the case with events. On the one hand, we want the event name to carry meaning. This helps us scale because by just looking at the event name and nothing else, there's meaning to be found. On the other hand, if try to overload the event name with too much meaning, the benefit of quickly deciphering event names is lost.

The primary focus of having good, short, and meaningful event names is on the developers who work with these events. The idea is that as their code is reacting to events, they can quickly put together a mental map of event flow. Mind you, this is just one small practice that contributes to the overall scalable event architecture, but nonetheless it is an important one.

For example, we might have a base event type, and a more specific version of that event. We could have several of these base event types, and several more specific instances of them to cover the more direct scenarios. If we have too much specificity with our event-names and types, it means we can't really reuse them. It also means there are more events for developers to reason with.

Data format

Apart from the event name itself, there's the event payload. This should always contain data about the event that's triggered, and possibly data about the components that trigger them. The most important thing to keep in mind about event data is that it should always have data that's pertinent to the handlers that subscribe to these types of events. Often, a callback function may decide to do nothing and ignore the event, based on the state of a property in the event data.

For example, it's not really scalable if in every callback function we have to perform lookups on components, just to get the data we need to make a decision or perform further actions. It's not easy, of course, to guess what data is going to be required. If we knew this, we would just call the function directly, and save the hassle of having an event triggering mechanism to begin with. The idea is to loosen coupling, but at the same time, provide data that's predictable.

Here's a simplified example of what event data might look like:

```
var eventData = {
    type: 'app.click',
    timestamp: new Date(),
    target: 'button.next'
};
```

A useful exercise for trying to figure out which data is relevant for a given event when it's triggered, is to think about what can be derived from within the handler, and what the handler almost never needs. For example, it's not advised to compute event data, and then pass it around. If the handler can compute it, it should probably bear that responsibility. If we start seeing repetitive code, then that's a different story and it's time to start thinking about common event data.

Common data

Event data will always contain data from the component that triggered the event — possibly a reference to the component itself. That's always a good bet, since all we know today is that the event was triggered — we have no idea what callbacks are going to want to do in response to this event later on. So it's good to give our callback functions lots of data, so long as it's not confusing or misleading.

So if we know that the same type of component will always trigger the same types of events, we can design our callbacks accordingly with the expectation that the same data will always be there. We can get even more generic with our event data, and supply the callbacks with data about the event itself. For example, there are things like time stamps, event-state, and so on — these have nothing to do with the component, and more to do with the event.

Here's an example that shows a base event that defines the common data for all events that extend it with additional properties:

```
// click-event.js
// All instances will have "type" and "timestamp"
// properties, plus any passed-in properties. What's
// important is that anything using "ClickEvent"
// knows that "type" and "timestamp" will always be
```

```
// there.
export default class ClickEvent {

    constructor(properties) {
        this.type = 'app.click';
        this.timestamp = new Date();
        Object.assign(this, properties);
    }

};

// main.js
import ClickEvent from 'click-event.js';

// Create a new "ClickEvent" and pass it some properties.
// We can override some of the standard properties,
// and pass it new ones.
var clickEvent = new ClickEvent({
    type: 'app.button.click',
    target: 'button.next',
    moduleState: 'enabled'
});

console.log(clickEvent);
```

Again, don't try to be clever about data reuse upfront. Let the repetitiveness happen, and then deal with it. The better approach would be to create a base event structure, so that it's easy to move repetitive properties into the common structure once they've been 'found.

Traceable component communication

Perhaps the biggest challenge with large-scale JavaScript applications is keeping a mental-model of where events start and where they end, in other words, tracing the event as it flows through our components. Untraceable code puts the scalability of our software at risk because we cannot predict what will happen in response to a given event.

There are a number of tactics we can use during development to ease the pain of figuring out our event flow, perhaps even modifying the design to simplify things. Simplicity scales, and we can't simplify what we don't understand.

Subscribing to events

One nice aspect of the publish-subscribe messaging model is that we can jump in and add a new subscription. This means that if we're not sure about how something works, we can throw event callback functions at the problem from various angles, until we have a better idea of what's actually happening. This is a hacker tool, and tools that support hacking our software help us scale because we're empowering developers to take matters into their own hands. If something isn't clear, they're more likely to figure it out on their own when the code is easy to hack.

Subscribing to events at specific points, or in a specific order, can alter the lifecycle of the event. It's important to have this ability, but if it is overused, it can lead to unnecessary complexity

In drastic cases, we might even need to use this subscriber approach to fix something that's broken in a production system. For example, say that a callback function is able to stop an event from executing, canceling any further handlers from running. It's good to have these types of entry points in the events that trigger throughout our code.

Globally-logging events

The callback functions that execute in response to triggered events can log messages from within. There are times, however, when we need logging from the perspective of the event mechanism itself. For example, if we're dealing with some tricky code, and we need to know when our callback function is being called, relative to other callback functions. The event triggering mechanism should have an option to handle lifecycle logging.

This means that for any given event that's triggered, we can see information logged about the event, independent of the code that runs in response to the event. We'll call these meta-events — events about events. For example, the trigger time before the callback runs, after the callback runs, and when there are no more callbacks. This gives the logging we implement in our callbacks some much-needed context for tracing our code.

Following is an example that shows an event broker with logging enabled:

```
// events.js
// A simple event broker.
export default class Events {

    // Accepts a "log()" function when created,
```

```
                // used when triggering events.
                constructor(log) {
                    this.log = log;
                    this.listeners = {};
                }

                // Calls all functions listening to event "name", passing
                // "data" to each. If the "log()" function was provided to
                // the broker when created, then it logs BEFORE each callback
                // is called, and AFTER.
                trigger(name, data) {
                    if (name in this.listeners) {
                        var log = this.log;
                        return this.listeners[name].map(function(callback) {
                            log && console.log('BEFORE', name);

                            var result = callback(Object.assign({
                                name: name
                            }, data));

                            log && console.log('AFTER', name);

                            return result;
                        });
                    }
                }
            };

// main.js
import Events from 'events.js';

// Two event callback functions that log
// data. The second one is async because it
// uses "setTimeout()".
function callbackFirst(data) {
    console.log('CALLBACK', data.name);
}

function callbackLast(data) {
    setTimeout(function() {
        console.log('CALLBACK', data.name);
    }, 500);
}
```

```
var broker = new Events(true);

broker.listen('first', callbackFirst);
broker.listen('last', callbackLast);

broker.trigger('first');
broker.trigger('last');

//
// BEFORE first
// CALLBACK first
// AFTER first
// BEFORE last
// AFTER last
// CALLBACK last
//
// Notice how we can trace the event broker
// invocation? Also note that "CALLBACK last"
// is obviously async because it's not in between
// "BEFORE last" and "AFTER last".
```

Event lifecycle

Different event triggering mechanisms have different lifecycles for their events, and it's worthwhile trying to understand how each works, and how they can be controlled. We'll start by looking at DOM events. The DOM nodes in our UI form a tree structure, and any one of those nodes can trigger a DOM event. If there are handler functions for this event attached directly to the triggering node, they'll be executed. Then, the event will propagate upward, repeating the process of looking for handler functions, and then continuing up the tree until the document node is reached.

Our handler functions can actually change the default propagation behavior of DOM events.

For example, if we don't want handlers further up in the DOM tree to run, handlers in lower tree nodes can stop the event from propagating.

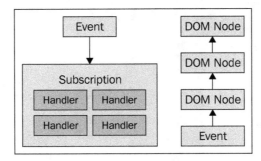

Contrasting the event processing approaches of the component event systems from various frameworks, and the DOM events as handled by the browser

The other major event triggering mechanism we'll want to pay attention to is that of the framework we're using. JavaScript, as a language, has no general purpose event triggering system, only specialized ones for DOM trees, Ajax calls, and Promise objects. Internally, these are all using the same task queues; they're just exposed in ways that make them seem as though they're separate systems. This is where the framework we're using steps in and provides the necessary abstraction. These types of event dispatchers are quite simple; subscribers for a given event are executed in FIFO order. Some of these event systems support more advanced lifecycle options discussed in this section, such as global event logging and early event termination.

Communication overhead

One advantage of directly invoking a method on a component is that there's very little overhead involved. When all inter-component communication is brokered through an event triggering mechanism, there's no way to escape at least a little overhead. In fact, overhead associated with this indirection is hardly noticeable; it's other overhead factors that can cause scalability issues.

In this section we'll look at event triggering frequency, callback execution, and callback complexity. Each of these has the potential to degrade the performance of our software to the point where it is unusable.

Event frequency

When our software has only a handful of components, there's a fundamental limit on the frequency of events. Where event frequency can quickly turn into a problem is when there are lots of components, some of which trigger events in response to events. This means that if the user is doing something quickly and efficiently, or if there are several Ajax responses arriving all at once, we need a way to prevent these events from blocking the DOM.

One challenge with JavaScript is that it's single-threaded. There are web workers, but those go way beyond the scope of this book because they introduce a whole new category of architectural issues. Let's say that the user has clicked something four times in under one second. Under normal circumstances, this is no big deal for our event system to process. But let's say they're doing this while there's an expensive Ajax response handler running. Eventually, the UI will become unresponsive.

To avoid unresponsive UIs, we can throttle our events. This means putting a cap on the callback execution frequency. So, instead of *done, onto the next one*, it's *done, rest for a few milliseconds, then onto the next one*. The advantage of throttling our callback functions like this is it gives pending DOM updates or pending DOM event callback functions a chance to run. The disadvantage is that our event lifecycle could be negatively impacted due to long-running updates, or other code.

Following is an example that shows an event broker that throttles triggered events to a specific time frequency:

```
// events.js
// The event broker. Sets sets the threshold
// for event triggering frequency to 100
// milliseconds.
export default class Events {

    constructor() {
        this.last = null;
        this.threshold = 100;
        this.size = 0;
        this.listeners = {};
    }

    // Triggers the event, but only if the it meets the
```

```
            // frequency threshold.
        trigger(name, data) {
            var now = +new Date();

            // If we're passed the wait threshold, or we've never
            // triggered an event, we can call "_trigger()", where
            // the event callback functions are processed.
            if (this.last === null || now - this.last > this.threshold) {
                this._trigger(name, data);
                this.last = now;
            // Otherwise, we've triggered something recently, and we
            // need to set a timeout. The "size" multiplier is
            // for spreading out the lineup of triggers.
            } else {
                this.size ++;
                setTimeout(() => {
                    this._trigger(name, data);
                    this.size --;
                }, this.threshold * this.size || 1);
            }
        }


        // This is the actual triggering mechanism, called by
        // "trigger()" after it checks the frequency threshold.
        _trigger(name, data) {
            if (name in this.listeners) {
                return this.listeners[name].map(function(callback) {
                    return callback(Object.assign({
                        name: name
                    }, data));
                    return result;
                });
            }
        }
    }
};

//main.js
import Events from 'events.js';

function callback(data) {
    console.log('CALLBACK', new Date().getTime());
}
```

```
var broker = new Events(true);

broker.listen('throttled', callback);

var counter = 5;

// Trigger events in a tight loop. This will
// cause the broker to throttle the callback
// processing.
while (counter--) {
    broker.trigger('throttled');
}
//
// CALLBACK 1427840290681
// CALLBACK 1427840290786
// CALLBACK 1427840290886
// CALLBACK 1427840290987
// CALLBACK 1427840291086
//
// Notice how the logged timestamps in each
// callback are spread out?
```

Callback execution time

While the event triggering mechanism has some level of control over when callback functions are executed, we don't necessarily control how long the callbacks will take to finish. From the event system's perspective, each callback function is a little black box that runs to completion, due to the single-threaded nature of JavaScript. If a disruptive callback function is thrown at the event mechanism, how do we know which callback is at fault, so that we can diagnose and fix it?

There are two techniques that can be used to address this problem. As mentioned earlier in the chapter, the event triggering mechanism should probably have an easy means to turn on global event logging. From there, we can deduce the duration of any given callback that's running, assuming we have the start and complete timestamps. But this isn't exactly the most efficient way to enforce callback duration times.

Another technique is to set a timeout function, once a given callback function starts running. When the timeout function runs, say after 1 second, it checks if the same callback is still running. If so, it can explicitly raise an exception. That way, the system explicitly fails when a callback takes too long.

There's still a problem with this approach—what if the callback is stuck in a tight loop? Our monitoring callback will never get an opportunity to run.

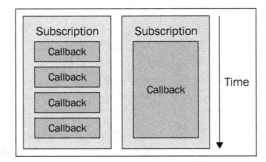

Comparing short callbacks that don't take long to execute with longer callbacks, which don't provide much flexibility for updating the DOM, or processing queued DOM events

Callback complexity

When all else fails, it's up to us, the architects of the large-scale JavaScript application, to make sure that the complexity of event handlers is at an appropriate level. Too much complexity means the potential for performance bottlenecks and the freezing of the UI—a bad user experience. If the callback functions are too fine-grained, or the events themselves for that matter, we still face a performance problem because of the added overhead of the event triggering mechanism itself—more callbacks to process mean more overhead.

What's nice about the event systems that are found in most JavaScript frameworks that support inter-component communications is that they're flexible. The frameworks will, by default, trigger events that it feels are important. These can be ignored at no observable performance cost to us. However, they also allow us to trigger our own events as need be. So if we find that after a while, we've gotten carried away with the granularity of our events, we can scale them back a little.

Once we have a grasp of what the right level of event granularity is for our application, we can adjust our callback functions to reflect it. We can even start writing our smaller callback functions in such a way that they can be used to compose higher-level functions that provide more course-grained functionality.

Here's an example that shows callback functions that trigger other events, and other more focused functions listening to these events:

```javascript
import Events from 'events.js';

// These callbacks trigger "logic" events. This
// small indirection keeps our logic decoupled
// from event handlers that might have to perform
// other boilerplate activities.
function callbackFirst(data) {
    data.broker.trigger('logic', {
        value: 'from first callback'
    });
}

function callbackSecond(data) {
    data.broker.trigger('logic', {
        value: 'from second callback'
    });
}

var broker = new Events();

broker.listen('click', callbackFirst);
broker.listen('click', callbackSecond);

// The "logic" callback is small, and focused. It
// doesn't have to worry about things like DOM
// access or fetching network resources.
broker.listen('logic', (data) => {
    console.log(data.name, data.value);
});

broker.trigger('click');
//
// logic from first callback
// logic from second callback
```

Areas of communication responsibility

When thinking about JavaScript component communication, it's helpful to look at the outside world, and the edges from which our application touches it. We've mostly been focused on inter-component communication thus far—how do our components talk to other components within the same JavaScript application? This inter-component communication doesn't initiate itself, nor does it end here. Scalable JavaScript code needs to consider the events that flow into and out of the application.

Backend API

The obvious starting point is the backend API, since it defines the domain of our application. The frontend is really just a facade for the ultimate truth of the API. Of course, it's more than that, but the API data does ultimately constrain what we can and cannot do with our application.

In terms of components and responsibilities, it's helpful to think about which ones are responsible for communicating directly with the backend. When the application needs data, it's these components that will initiate the API conversation, fetch this data, and let me know when it has arrived so that I can hand it off to another component. So there's actually quite a bit of inter-component communication that's indirectly related to components that talk to the API.

For example, let's say we have a collection component, and to populate it, we have to call a method. Does the collection know that it needs to populate itself, or create itself for that matter? It's more likely that some other component kicked-off the creation of the collection, then asked it to fetch some data from the API. While we know that this initiating component doesn't directly talk to the API, we also know that it plays an important role in the communication.

This is important to think about when scaling to lots of components because they should all follow a predictable pattern.

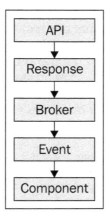

An event broker in the frontend, directly or indirectly, translates API responses and their data into events our components can subscribe to

Web socket updates

Web socket connections alleviate the need for long-polling in web applications. They're used more frequently now because there's strong browser support for the technology. There are a lot of libraries for backend servers to support web socket connections too. The challenging part is the book-keeping that allows us to detect a change and notify the relevant sessions by sending a message.

Backend complexities aside, web sockets do solve a lot of soft real time update problems in the frontend. Web sockets are a bi-directional communication channel with the backend, but where they really shine is in receiving updates, that some model has changed state.

This allows any of our components that might be displaying data from this model to re-render itself.

The challenging part is that in any given frontend session, we're only allowed one web socket connection. This means that our handler function that responds to these messages needs to figure out what to do with them. You may recall that, earlier in the chapter when we went over event data, and the meaningfulness of event names and the structure of their data. Web socket message events are a good example of why this matters. We need to figure out what to do with it, and there would be a lot of variation in the type of web socket messages we get.

 Since web socket connections are stateful, they can be dropped. This means that we will have to face the additional challenge of implementing code that reconnects dropped socket connections.

It would be a bad idea to let a single callback function handle all the processing of these web socket messages, right down to the DOM. One approach might be to have several handlers, one for each specific type of web socket update. This would get out of hand quickly because lots of callback functions would have to run, and in terms of responsibility, lots of components would have to be tightly coupled to the web socket connection.

What if the component doesn't care that the updated data came from a web socket connection? All it cares about is that the data changed. Perhaps we need to introduce a new type of event for the components that care about data changes. Then, our web socket handler will just need to translate the message to those types of events. This is a scalable approach to web socket communication, because we could rip out web sockets entirely and it wouldn't actually touch a lot of the system.

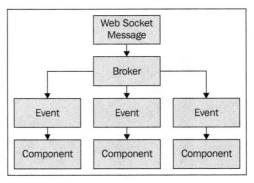

An event translates one type of web socket message into entity-specific events, so only the interested components need to subscribe

DOM updates

Our components need to interact with the DOM. This goes without saying — it's a web application that runs in the browser. It's definitely worth thinking about components that touch the DOM, and those that don't. These are often the **view** components, since they translate the data of our application into something that is viewable by the user in their browser window.

These types of components are actually more of a challenge to scale, mostly due to the bi-directional nature of their event flows. Adding to this challenge is the fact that when there's any doubt about where some new piece of code should go, it's usually the view. Then, when our views get overloaded, we start putting code in controllers, or utilities, and who knows where else. There has to be a better way.

Let's think about view event communication for a minute. First there are the incoming events. These tell the view that something has happened with our data and it should update the DOM. Obligingly, it does just that. This approach is actually really solid, and works well when the view listens to one component for events. As we scale our application to accommodate more features and enhancements, our views have to start figuring things out. Views work better when they're stupid.

For example, the view that initially had the responsibility of rendering one element in response to a data event, now has to do much more. After it's finished with this, it needs to compute some derived value, and update another element. This process of making views "smarter" spirals out of control until we can no longer scale.

From a communication perspective, we want to think of views as a simple one-to-one binding of data to DOM. If that principle is never violated, then it's a lot easier for us to predict what will happen when data changes, because we know which views will be listening to this data, and the DOM elements they're bound to.

Now for binding in the other direction — listening for changes in the DOM. The challenge here, again, is that we tend to lean toward making our views smart. When there's an issue with our input data, we overload the view event handler that's triggered in response to a DOM event with responsibilities that should be fulfilled elsewhere. Views work better when they're stupid. They should translate DOM events into application-specific events that any other component can listen to, just like we do with web socket message events. Our "smarter" components that actually initiate some business process don't necessarily care that the cause for action was from the DOM. This helps us scale by creating a smaller number of generic components, that really don't do much.

Loosely-coupled communication

When inter-component communication is loosely coupled, we can more easily adapt to scaling influencers when they arise. First and foremost, a good inter-component communication design that's event-driven allows us to move components around. We can take a faulty or under-performing component out, and replace it with another. Not being able to substitute components this way means that we would have to fix the component in-place; a larger risk for delivering software and a scaling bottleneck from a development perspective.

Another beneficial side-effect of loosely coupled inter-component communication is that we can isolate problematic components when something goes wrong. We can prevent exceptions that occur in one component from leaving other components in a bad state, which just leads to further problems when the user tries to do something else. Isolating problems like this helps us scale our responses to fix faulty components.

Substituting components

Based on the events a given component triggers and responds to, we should have an easy time substituting a component with a different version. We still need to figure out the inner workings of the component, because it's unlikely we want to change it completely. But that's the easier part—the difficult part of implementing components is wiring them together. Scalable component implementation means making this wiring as approachable and coherent as possible.

But why is it so important that components be substitutable? We would think that stable code, consisting of a handful of wired-together components wouldn't have to change all that often, if at all. From this point of view, of course substitutability is devalued—why worry about it if you don't use it? The only problem with this mindset is that if we take scaling our JavaScript code seriously, we can't apply principles to some components while neglecting others.

In fact, the reluctance to re-factor stable code isn't necessarily a good thing. For example, it could actually hold us back if we have some new ideas that would require us to re-factor stable components. What substitutability across all our components buys us is scalability in implementing new ideas. If it's easy to experiment by pulling out stable components and putting in new implementations, then we're more likely to put improved design ideas into the product.

Substituting components isn't just a design-time activity. We can introduce variability, where there will be a number of possible components that could fill a gap, and the right component will be chosen at runtime. This flexibility means that we can easily extend features to account for scaling influencers, such as new user roles.

Some roles get one component, others get a different but compatible component, or no component at all. The key is to support this flexibility.

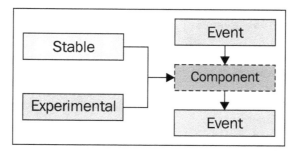

As long as components follow the same communication protocols, usually with event triggering and handling, developing experimental technology is easier

Handling unexpected events

Loosely coupled components help us scale our ability to address defective components, mainly because when we're able to isolate the problem root to a single component, we can quickly pinpoint the problem and fix it. Additionally, in the case where the defective component is running in a production environment, we can limit the negative impact while we implement and deliver the fix.

Defects happen—we need to accept this and design for it. We want to learn from defects when they happen so that we don't repeat them in the future. Given that we're on a tight schedule, releasing early and often, bugs will slip through the cracks. These are edge cases that we haven't tested for, or unique programming errors that slipped through our unit tests. Regardless, we need to design our component failure modes to account for these circumstances.

One approach to isolating defective components might be to wrap any event callback functions in a try/catch. If any unexpected exception happens, our callback simply notifies the event system about the component being in an error state. This gives the other handlers a chance to restore their states. If there's a faulty component in the event callback pipeline, we can safely display an error to the user about that particular action not working. Since the other components are all in a good state, thanks to the notification from the bad component, the user can safely use other features.

Following is an example that shows an event broker capable of catching callback function errors:

```javascript
// events.js
export default class Events {

    constructor() {
        this.listeners = {};
    }

    // Triggers an event...
    trigger(name, data) {
        if (!(name in this.listeners)) {
            return;
        }

        // We need this to keep track of the error state.
        var error = false,
            mapped;

        mapped = this.listeners[name].map((callback) => {
            // If the previous callback caused an error,
            // we don't run any more callbacks. The values
            // in the mapped output will be "undefined".
            if (error) {
                return;
            }

            var result;

            // Catch any exceptions thrown by the callback function,
            // and the result object sets "error" to true.
            try {
                result = callback(Object.assign({
                    name: name,
                    broker: this
                }, data));
            } catch (err) {
                result = { error: true };
            }

            // The callbacks can throw an exception, or just return
            // an object with the "error" property set to true. The
            // outcome is the same - we stop processing callbacks.
```

```
            if (result && result.error) {
                error = true;
            }

            return result;
        });

        // Something went wrong, so we let other components know
        // by triggering an error variant of the event.
        if (error) {
            this.trigger('${name}:error');
        }
    }
}


// main.js
import Events from 'events.js';

// Callback fails by returning an error object.
function callbackError(data) {
    console.log('callback:', 'going to return an error');
    return { error: true };
}


// Callback fails by throwing an exception.
function callbackException(data) {
    console.log('callback:', 'going to raise an exception');
    throw Error;
}


var broker = new Events();

// Listens to both the regular events (the happy path),
// and the error variants.
broker.listen('shouldFail', callbackError);
broker.listen('shouldFail:error', () => {
    console.error('error returned from callback');
});

broker.listen('shouldThrow', callbackException);
broker.listen('shouldThrow:error', () => {
    console.error('exception thrown from callback');
});
```

```
broker.trigger('shouldFail');
broker.trigger('shouldThrow');
// callback: going to return an error
// error returned from callback
// callback: going to raise an exception
// exception thrown from callback
```

Component layers

There's a threshold within any sufficiently large JavaScript application, where the number of communicating components presents a scaling problem. The main bottleneck is the complexity we create, and our inability to understand it. To fight against this complexity, we can introduce layers. These are abstract categorical notions that help us visually understand what's happening at runtime.

Event flow direction

One of the first things designing with layers will reveal about our code, is the complexity of our inter-component communication in terms of event flow direction. For example, let's say our application has three layers. The top layer is concerned with routing, and other entry points into the UI. The middle layer has data and business logic spread throughout. The bottom layer is where our views are found. It's not about how many components are in these layers; while that's a factor, it's a minor one. What's important from this perspective is the types of arrows that cross into other layers.

For example, given the three-layered architecture described above, we would probably notice that the most straightforward layer connections are between the routers and the data/business logic layer. That's because the events flow mostly in one direction: top down, from router to the layer directly beneath it. From there, there's likely some communication that happens between some model and controller components, but then ultimately, the event flow keeps moving downward.

Between the data/logic layer and the view layer, the communication arrows start to look bi-directional and confusing. That's because the event flows in the code are also bi-directional and confusing. This isn't scalable because we can't easily grasp the effects of the events we're triggering. What's helpful for using the layered design approach is figuring out a way to remove bi-directional event flows. This probably means introducing a level of indirection, something that's responsible for brokering the event between a source and a target.

If we do this in a clever way, the additional moving part brings clarity instead of clutter to our layer diagram, and the performance impact is negligible.

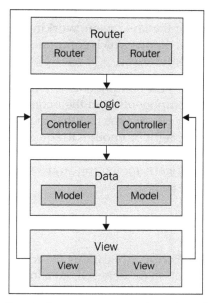

A discernible event flow direction between component layers has a huge impact on scalability

Mapping to developer responsibilities

Layers are an aid, not a formal architecture specification artifact. This means that we can use them for whatever they might be helpful with. Different groups of people might have their own layers that they use for purposes that suit their needs in understanding complexity. However, it's more useful if the development team as a whole follows the same layers, and that they're kept extremely simple. Going beyond four or five layers defeats the purpose of using them.

Developers can use layers as a means of self-organization. They understand the architecture, and they have work to do for the upcoming sprint. Let's say we have two developers working on the same feature. They can use the layers of our component architecture to plan their implementation, and avoid interfering with each other's work. Things just come together seamlessly when there's a point of reference in the bigger picture, such as a layer.

Mentally mapping the code

Even without diagrams, just knowing that the component code we're looking at belongs in a specific layer, helps us to mentally map what it's doing, and it's effect on the rest of the system. Knowing the layer we're working in gives us a subconscious context while we're coding—we know which components are our neighbors, and when our events cross layer boundaries.

Framed in the context of a layer, new components will have glaringly obvious design problems, relative to existing components, and their communication patterns between layers. The existence of these layers, and the fact that they're frequently used as an informal aid by all developers, might be enough to squash design issues early on. Or maybe there's not really an issue, but the layers are enough to promote discussion on design. Some of the team might learn something, and some might walk away with self-assurance that the design is solid.

Summary

The building blocks of our JavaScript applications are components. The glue that holds them together is the communication model used. At a low level, inter-component communication consists of one component passing a message to another, through a broker mechanism of some sort. This is often abstracted and simplified as an event system.

We looked at what actually gets passed around from one component to the next in the form of event data. This data needs to be consistent, predictable, and meaningful. We also looked at traceable events. That is, can we globally log events as they're triggered from the event triggering mechanism?

The boundaries of our JavaScript code are communication endpoints. We looked at the various components with responsibilities of communication with external systems, like the DOM, Ajax calls, or local storage. We need to insulate our smart components from the edges of our system.

Substitutability and layers are crucial concepts for scaling. Replacing components helps us scale by quickly developing new code with little risk. Layers help in a number of areas by keeping the bigger picture within reach. Incorrect design assumptions are exposed earlier on with layers.

Now it's time for us to think about scaling the addressability of our application, and we'll see if the lessons from the last two chapters are of any value there.

Addressability and Navigation

5

Applications that live on the web rely on **addressable** resources. The URI is an essential internet technology. It eliminates a whole class of complexity, because we can encode bits of information about resources into URI strings. That's the *policy* part. The *mechanism* part is up to the browser, or our JavaScript code—looking up the requested resource and displaying it.

In the past, processing URIs took place in the backend. The browser's responsibility, when the user passed it a URI, was to send this request to the backend and display the response. With large-scale JavaScript applications, this responsibility has shifted mostly to the frontend. We have the tools to implement sophisticated routing in the browser, and with that, there's less reliance on backend-technologies.

The benefits of frontend routing do come at a cost, however, once our software packs on features. This chapter takes a deep look into the routing scenarios that we're likely to encounter as our application architecture grows and matures. Most low-level implementation specifics of router components from frameworks, aren't important. We're more concerned with how well our router components adapt to scaling influencers.

Approaches to routing

There are two approaches to routing in JavaScript. The first is using hash-based URIs. These are the URIs that begin with the # character and this is the more popular approach. The other less popular approach is to use the history API of the browser to generate more traditional URIs the web population is used to. This technique is more involved, and has only recently gained enough browser support to make it viable.

Hash URIs

The hash portion of the URI was originally intended to point to a specific location in the document. So the browser would look at everything to the *left* of the # character, and send this information to the backend, asking for some page content. Only when the page arrived and was rendered did the *right* side of the # character become relevant. This is when the browser used the hash portion of the URI to find the locally relevant spot within the page.

Today, the hash portion of the URI is used differently. It's still used to avoid passing irrelevant data to the backend when the URI changes. The main difference is that today we're dealing with applications and features instead of web sites and static content. Since most of the application is already loaded into the browser when the address changes, it doesn't make sense to send unnecessary requests to backend. We only want the data that we need for the new URI, and that's usually accomplished with an API request in the background.

When we talk about using the hash approach to URIs in JavaScript applications and changing the URI, it's usually only the hash portion that changes. This means that the relevant browser events will fire, notifying our code that the URI changed. But it won't automatically issue a request to the backend for new page content, and this is key. We can actually get a lot of performance and efficiency gains out of frontend routing like this, and that's one of the reasons we use this approach.

Not only does it work well, but it's easy to implement. There's not a lot of moving parts in implementing a hash change event listener that executes logic to fetch the relevant data, and then updates the page with the relevant content. Further, the browser history changes are automatically handled for us.

Traditional URIs

For some users and developers, the hash approach just feels like a hack. Not to mention the SEO challenges presented in a public internet setting. They prefer the look and feel of the more traditional slash-separated resource name format. That's generally possible to achieve now in all modern browsers, thanks to enhancements to the history API. Essentially, the routing mechanism can listen for states being pushed onto the history stack, and when that happens, it prevents the request from being sent to the backend, and instead processes it locally.

There's obviously more code required for this approach to work, and more edge cases to think about. For example, the backend needs to support all the URIs that the frontend router does, because the user can feed any valid URI into the application. One technique to deal with this is a rewrite rule on the server that redirects 404 errors back to the application index page, where our real route processing lives.

That said, the router components found in most JavaScript application frameworks abstract the differences in approach and provide a means to seamlessly go in one direction or another. Does it matter which one is used, either for enhanced functionality or improved scalability? Not really. But in terms of scalability, it's important to acknowledge that there are in fact two main approaches, and that we don't want to commit ourselves entirely to one over the other.

How routers work

Now it's time for us to dig a little deeper into routers. We want to know the responsibilities of a router, and what it's lifecycle looks like when the URI changes. Essentially, this amounts to the router taking the new URI and figuring out if it's something the router is interested in. If it is, then it triggers the appropriate route events with the parsed URI data as arguments.

Understanding the role of routers at a low-level is important for scaling our application because the more URIs we have, and the more components we have responding to these route events, the more potential for scaling issues. When we know what's happening with the router lifecycle, we can make the appropriate scaling trade-offs in response to scaling influencers.

Router responsibilities

A simplistic view of a router is just a map—there's routes, string or regular expression pattern definitions, which map to callback functions. What's important is that this process is fast, predictable, and stable. This is challenging to get right, especially as the number of URIs in our application grow. Here's a rough approximation of what any router component needs to handle:

- Storing a mapping of route patterns to their corresponding event names
- Listening to URI change events—*hash change* or *pop state*
- Performing the route pattern lookup, comparing the new URI to each mapped pattern

- When a match is found, to parse the new URI according to the pattern
- Triggering the mapped route event, passing any parsed data

The route lookup process involves a linear search through the route map to find a match. This can mean significant performance degradation when there's lots of routes defined. When the route mapping is an array of objects, it can also lead to inconsistent router performance. For example, if a route is at the end of the array, it means it's checked last and performs slowly. If it's at the beginning of the array, it performs better.

To avoid performance degradation in frequently accessed URIs, we could extend the router so that it sorts the route map array by a priority property. Another approach would involve using a **trie** structure, to avoid linear lookups. Of course, only consider optimizations like these if there are so many routes that the router performance is measurably poor.

The router has a lot to do when the URI changes, which is why it's important to understand the lifecycle of a given route, from the time the URI changes in the address bar, to the completion of all it's event handler functions. From a performance perspective, lots of routes can negatively impact our application. From a composition perspective, it's challenging to keep track of what components create and react to which routes. This is a little easier to handle when we know what the lifecycle of any given route looks like.

Router events

Once the router has found a match for the changed URI, and once it has parsed the URI according to its matching pattern, its final job is to trigger the route event. The event that's triggered is supplied as part of the mapping. The URI may encode variables, and these get parsed and passed to each router event handler as data.

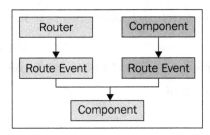

Route events provide an abstraction layer, which means that components that aren't routers can trigger route events

Most frameworks ship with router components that can directly call a function in response to a route change, instead of triggering a route event. This is actually easier, and is a more direct approach that makes sense with smaller applications. The indirection we get by triggering events from the router through the event triggering mechanism is that our components are loosely coupled to the router.

This is beneficial because different components that have no knowledge of one another can listen to the same route event. As we scale, the same routes that have been in place for a while will need to take on new responsibilities, and it's easier to add new handlers than it is to keep building upon the same function code. There's also the abstraction benefit—the components that listen to route events don't care that the event is actually triggered by a router instance. This is useful when we need a component to trigger router-like behavior, without actually having to depend on the router.

URI parts and patterns

With large scale JavaScript applications, a lot of thought goes into the router component. We also need to put a lot of thought into the URIs themselves. What are they composed of? Are they consistent throughout the application? What makes a bad URI? Veering in the wrong direction on any of these considerations makes scaling the addressability of our application difficult.

Encoding information

The point of a URI is that a client can just pass it to our application, and it contains enough information that something useful can be done with it. The simplest URI just points to a resource type, or a static location within an app—/users or /home are respective examples of these types of URIs. Using this information, our router can trigger a route event, and a callback function is triggered. These callbacks wouldn't even require any arguments—they just know what to do because there's no variability.

On the other hand, router callback functions may need a bit of context. This is when encoding information within a URI becomes important. The most common use for this is when the client asks for a specific instance of some resource, using a unique identifier. For example, `users/31729`. Here, the router will need to find a pattern that matches this string, and the pattern will also specify how to extract the `31729` variable. This is then passed to the callback function, which now has enough context information to perform it's task.

URIs can grow large and complex if we try to encode lots of information in them. An example of this would be encoding query parameters for a page that displays a grid of resources. Trying to specify all the possibilities in the route pattern is difficult and error-prone. There are bound to be changes, and unanticipated edge-cases concerning the combinations used with the variables. Some will likely be optional.

When a given URI has this much potential for complexity, it's best to keep the encoding options out of the URI pattern that's passed to the router. Instead, have the callback function look at the URI and perform further parsing to figure out the context. That keeps the route specifications neat and tidy, and the odd complex handler isolated from everything else.

For common queries, we may want to provide a simple URI for our users, especially if it's presented as a link. For example, recent posts would link to /posts/recent. The handler for this URI has a few things that it needs to figure out that would otherwise need to be encoded in the URI—such as ordering and the number of resources to fetch. Sometimes these things don't need to be included in the URI, and decisions like these can benefit both the user experience and the scalability of our code.

Designing URIs

Resource names are a good inspiration for the URIs we create. If the URI links to a page that displays events, it should probably start with events. Sometimes, however, the resources exposed by the backend have anything but intuitive names. Or, as an organization or an industry, we like to abbreviate certain terms. These should be avoided as well, except in the case where the context of the application provides meaning.

The inverse is true as well—adding too much meaning in the URI can actually cause confusion, if it's too verbose. This can be too verbose from the individual word point of view, or from the number of URI components point of view. To help convey structure and make it easier for human eyes to parse, URIs are usually broken down into parts. For example, the type of thing, followed by the identifier of the thing. It's not really helpful to the user to encode categorical or other tangential information in the URI—it can certainly be displayed in the UI though.

Where we can, we should be consistent. If we're limiting the number of characters for a resource name, they should all follow the same limit. If we're using slashes to separate URI parts, it should be done the same everywhere. The whole idea behind this is that it scales nicely for our users when there are a lot of URIs, as they can eventually guess what a URI for something is, without having to click on a link.

While being consistent, we sometimes want certain types of URIs to stand out. For example, when we visit a page that puts a resource in a different state, or requires input from the user, we should prefix the action with a different symbol. Let's say we're editing a task—the URI might be /tasks/131:edit. We're being consistent everywhere in our application, separating our URI components with slashes. So we could have done something like /tasks/131/edit. However, this makes it seem as though it's a different resource when really, it's the same resource as tasks/131. Only now, the UI controls are in a different state.

Following is an example that shows some regular expressions used to test routes:

```
// Wildcards are used to match against parameters in URIs...
console.log('second', (/^user\/(.*)/i).exec('user/123'));
//     [ 'user/123', '123' ]

// Matches against the same URI, only more restrictively...
console.log('third', (/^user\/(\d+)/i).exec('user/123'));
//     [ 'user/123', '123' ]

// Doesn't match, looking for characters and we got numbers...
console.log('fourth', (/^user\/([a-z])/i).test('user/123'));
//     false

// Matches, we got a range of characters...
console.log('fifth', (/^user\/([a-z]+)/i).exec('user/abc'));
//     [ 'user/abc', 'abc' ]
```

Mapping resources to URIs

It's time to look at URIs in action. The most common form we'll find URIs in, are as links inside our application. At least, that's the idea; to have an application that's well connected. While the router understands what to do with URIs, we are yet to look at all the places where these links need to be generated and inserted into the DOM.

There are two approaches to generate links. The first is a somewhat manual process that requires the help of template engines and utility functions. The second takes a more automated approach in an attempt to scale the manageability of many URIs.

Building URIs manually

If a component renders content in the DOM, it potentially builds URI strings and adds them to link elements. This is easy enough to do when there's only a handful of pages and URIs. The scaling issue here is that the page count and URI count found in JavaScript applications are complimentary—lots of URIs means lots of pages and vice-versa.

We can use the router pattern mapping configuration, the structure that specifies what URIs look like and what happens when they're activated, as a reference when implementing our views. With the help of a template engine, which most frameworks use in one form or another, we can use the template features to dynamically render links as required. Or, lacking template sophistication, we'll need a standalone utility that can generate these URI strings for us.

This gets to be challenging when there are a lot of URIs to link, and a lot of templates. We have at least some help from the template syntax, which makes building these links a little less painful. But it's still time consuming and error-prone. Additionally, we'll start to see duplicative template content, thanks to the static nature of how we build links in the templates. We need to hard-code, at the very least, the type of resource we're linking to.

Automating resource URIs

The vast majority of the resources we link to are actual resources from the API, and are represented by a model or collection in our code. That being the case, it would be nice if instead of leveraging template tools to build URIs for these resources, we could use the same function on every model or collection to build the URI. That way, any duplication in our templates associated with building URIs goes away because we only care about the abstract `uri()` function.

This approach, while simplifying the templates, introduces a challenge with synchronizing the model with the router. For example, the URI string that's generated by the model needs to match the pattern that the router is expecting to see. So either, the implementer needs to be disciplined enough to keep the URI generation of the model in sync with the router, or the model somehow needs to base how it generates the URI string on the pattern.

If the router uses some kind of simplified regular expression syntax for building URI patterns, it's possible to keep the `uri()` function implemented by the model automatically synced by the route definition. The challenge there is that the model needs to know about the router—which can present a dependency scaling issue—we sometimes want models and not necessarily the router. What if our model stored the URI pattern that gets registered with the router? Then it could use this pattern to generate URI strings, and it's still only ever changed in one place. Another component would then register the pattern with the router, so there's no tight coupling with the model.

Following is an example that shows how the URI strings can be encapsulated in models, away from other components:

```
// router.js
import events from 'events.js';

// The router is also an event broker...
export default class Router {

    constructor() {
        this.routes = [];
    }

    // Adds a given "pattern" and triggers event "name"
    // when activated.
    add(pattern, name) {
        this.routes.push({
            pattern: new RegExp('^' +
                pattern.replace(/:\w+/g, '(.*)')),
            name: name
        });
    }

    // Adds any configured routes, and starts listening
    // for navigation events.
    start() {
        var onHashChange = () => {
            for (let route of this.routes) {
                let result = route.pattern.exec(
                    location.hash.substr(1));
                if (result) {
                    events.trigger('route:' + route.name, {
                        values: result.splice(1)
```

```
                });
                break;
            }
        }
    };

    window.addEventListener('hashchange', onHashChange);
    onHashChange();
    }

}

// model.js
export default class Model {

    constructor(pattern, id) {
        this.pattern = pattern;
        this.id = id;
    }

    // Generates the URI string for this model. The pattern is
    // passed in as a constructor argument. This means that code
    // that needs to generate URI strings, like DOM manipulation
    // code, can just ask the model for the URI.
    get uri() {
        return '#' + this.pattern.replace(/:\w+/, this.id);
    }

}

// user.js
import Model from 'model.js';

export default class User extends Model {

    // The URI pattern for instances of this model is
    // encapsulated in this static method.
    static pattern() {
        return 'user/:id';
    }

    constructor(id) {
        super(User.pattern(), id);
```

```
        }

}

// group.js
import Model from 'model.js';

export default class Group extends Model {

    // The "pattern()" method is static because
    // all instances of "Group" models will use the
    // same route pattern.
    static pattern() {
        return 'group/:id';
    }

    constructor(id) {
        super(Group.pattern(), id);
    }

}

// main.js
import Router from 'router.js';
import events from 'events.js';
import User from 'user.js';
import Group from 'group.js';

var router = new Router()

// Add routes using the "pattern()" static method. There's
// no need to hard-code any routes here.
router.add(User.pattern(), 'user');
router.add(Group.pattern(), 'group');

// Setup functions that respond to routes...
events.listen('route:user', (data) => {
    console.log(`User ${data.values[0]} activated`);
});

events.listen('route:group', (data) => {
    console.log(`Group ${data.values[0]} activated`);
```

```
        });

        // Construct new models, and user their "uri" property
        // in the DOM. Again, nothing related to routing patterns
        // need to be hard-coded here.
        var user = new User(1);
        document.querySelector('.user').href = user.uri;

        var group = new Group(1);
        document.querySelector('.group').href = group.uri;

        router.start();
```

Triggering routes

The most common route trigger is in the form of a user clicking a link within our application. As discussed in the preceding section, we need to equip our link generating mechanism to handle many pages, and many URIs. Another dimension of this scaling influencer is the actual triggering actions themselves. For instance, with smaller applications, there are obviously fewer links. So this also translates to fewer click events from the user — more navigation choices means higher event triggering frequency.

It's also important to consider the lesser known navigation actors. These include redirecting the user in response to some backend task completing, or just a straight-up work-around, to get from point A to point B.

User actions

When the user clicks a link in our application, the browser picks this up and changes the URI. This includes the entry point into our application — maybe from another web site or from a bookmark. This is what makes links and URIs so flexible, they can come from anywhere and point to anything. It makes sense to utilize links where we can because it means that our application is well connected, and processing a URI change is something our router excels at and can handle with ease.

But there're other ways to trigger URI changes and the subsequent router workflow. For example, let's say we're on a create event form. We submit the form, and the response comes back successful — do we want to leave the user at the create event page? Or do we want to take them to the page that shows the list of events, so they can see the event they just added? In the latter case, manually changing the URI makes sense and is very easy to implement.

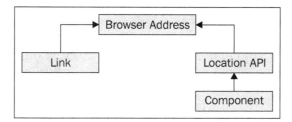

The different ways our application can change the address bar

Redirecting users

Redirecting users to a new route as the result of a successful API response is a good example of manually triggering the router. There are several other scenarios where we would want to redirect the user from where they currently are to a new page that coincides with the activity they're performing, or to make sure they're simply observing the correct information.

Not all heavy processing need happen in the backend — we could be faced with a local JavaScript component that runs a process, and upon completion, we want to take the user to another page within our app.

The key idea here is that the effect is more important than the cause — we don't care so much about what causes the URI change. What really matters is the ability to use the router in unforeseen ways. As our application scales, we'll be faced with scenarios where the way out is usually by a quick and simple router hack. Having total control over the navigation of our application gives us much more control over the way our application scales.

Router configuration

The mapping of our routes to their events is often lager than the router implementation itself. That's because as our application grows and acquires more route patterns, the list of possibilities gets bigger. A lot of the time, this is an unavoidable consequence of an application that's meeting its scaling demands. The trick is to not let a large number of route declarations collapse under their own weight, and this can happen in a number of ways.

There's more than one approach to configuring the routes that a given router instance responds to. Depending on the framework we're using, the router component may have more flexibility in how they're configured than others. Generally speaking, there's the static route approach, or the event registration approach. We'll also want to consider the router's ability to disable a given route at any given time.

Static route declarations

Simple applications usually configure their routers with a static declaration. This usually means a mapping of route patterns to callback functions, all at router creation time. What's nice about this approach is the relative locality of all the route patterns. At a glance, we can see what's happening with our route configuration, and we don't have to go hunting for specific route. However, this doesn't work is when there are lots of routes because we have to search for them. Also, there's no separation of concerns, and this doesn't play well with developers trying to do their thing independently of each other.

Registration events

When there are a lot of routes to define, the focus should be on encapsulated routes—which components need these routes, and how do they tell the router about them? Well, most routers will allow us to simply call a method that lets us add a new route configuration. Then we just need to include the router and add the routes from the component.

This is definitely a step in the right direction; it allows us to keep the route declarations in the components that need them, rather than kludging together an entire applications' worth of route configurations into a single object. However, we can take this scalability a step further.

Rather than having our components directly depend on a router instance, why not trigger an add route event? This will get picked up by any router that's listening for the event. Perhaps our application is using multiple router instances, each of which have their own specializations—logging, say—and they can all listen for added routes based on specific criteria. The point is, our components shouldn't have to care about the router instance, only that something is going to trigger route events when a given pattern matches against a URI change.

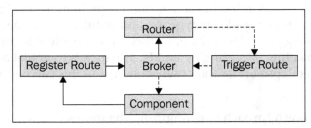

How to keep components isolated from routers by using events

Deactivating routes

After we've configured a given route, do we assume that it'll always be a viable route throughout the duration of the session? Or, should the router have some means to deactivate a given route? It depends on how we look at specific cases from a responsibility perspective.

For example, if something has happened, and some route should no longer be accessible—trying it just results in a user-friendly error—the route handler function can check whether the route is accessible or not. However, this adds complexity to the callback functions themselves, and this complexity will be sprinkled throughout the application in callbacks, rather than being self-contained in one place.

An alternative approach would be to have some sanity-checking component that deactivates routes when components enter states that warrant doing so. This same component would also enable routes when the state changes into something the route can handle.

A third approach would be to add a guard function as an option when the route is first registered. When the route is matched, it runs through this function, and if it passes the guard, then it is activated normally, otherwise, it fails. This approach scales best because the state that's checked; is tightly coupled with the relevant route, and there's no need to toggle between enabled/disabled states for routes. Think of a guard function as part of the matching criteria for routes.

Following is an example that shows a router that accepts guard condition functions. Route events aren't triggered if this guard function exists and returns false:

```
// router.js
import events from 'events.js';

// The router triggers events in response to
// route changes.
export default class Router {

    constructor() {
        this.routes = [];
    }

    // Adds a new route, with an optional
    // guard function.
    add(pattern, name, guard) {
        this.routes.push({
            pattern: new RegExp('^' +
```

```
                    pattern.replace(/:\w+/g, '(.*)')),
            name: name,
            guard: guard
        });
    }


    start() {
        var onHashChange = () => {
            for (let route of this.routes) {
                let guard = route.guard;
                let result = route.pattern.exec(
                    location.hash.substr(1));

                // If a match is found, and there's a guard
                // condition, evaluate it. The event is only
                // triggered if this passes.
                if (result) {
                    if (typeof guard === 'function' && guard()) {
                        events.trigger('route:' + route.name, {
                            values: result.splice(1)
                        });
                    }
                    break;
                }
            }
        };

        window.addEventListener('hashchange', onHashChange);
        onHashChange();
    }

}

// main.js
import Router from 'router.js';
import events from 'events.js';

var router = new Router()

// Function that can be used as a guard condition
// with any route we declare. It's returning a random
// value to demonstrate the various outcomes, but this
```

```
// could be anything that we want applied to all our routes.
function isAuthorized() {
    return !!Math.round(Math.random());
}

// The first route doesn't have a guard condition,
// and will always trigger a route event. The second
// route will only trigger a route event if the given
// callback function returns true.
router.add('open', 'open');
router.add('guarded', 'guarded', isAuthorized);

events.listen('route:open', () => {
    console.log('open route is always accessible');
});

events.listen('route:guarded', (data) => {
    console.log('made it past the guard function!');
});

router.start();
```

Troubleshooting routers

Once our routers grow to a sufficiently large size, we'll have to troubleshoot complex scenarios. If we know what the likely issues are beforehand, we'll be better equipped to deal with them. We can also build troubleshooting tools into our router instances to aid in the process. Scaling the addressability of our architecture means responding to issues quickly and predictably.

Conflicting routes

Conflicting routes can cause a massive headache because they can be really tricky to track down. A conflicting pattern is a general or similar version of more specific patterns added to the router later on. The more general pattern conflicts, because it's matched against the most specific URIs, which should have been matched by the more specific patterns. However, they're never tested because the general route is executed first.

When this happens, it may not be apparent at all that there's an issue with the routing because the incorrect route handler will run perfectly fine, and in the UI, everything will seem normal—except for one thing that's slightly off. If routes are processed in FIFO order, specificity matters. That is, if the more general route patterns are added first, then they'll always match against the more specific URI strings, as they're activated.

The challenge with ordering URIs like this when there's lots of them, is that it's time-consuming work. We have to compare the ordering of any new routes we may add to the patterns of existing routes. There's also the potential for conflicts between developer commitments if they're all being added to the same place. This is another advantage of separating routes by component. It makes potentially conflicting routes a lot easier to spot and deal with, because the component likely has a small number of similar URI patterns.

Following is an example that shows a router component with two conflicting routes:

```javascript
// Finds the first matching route in "routes" - tested
// against "uri".
function match() {
    for (let route of routes) {
        if (route.route.test(uri)) {
            console.log('match', route.name);
            break;
        }
    }
}

var uri = 'users/abc';

var routes = [
    { route: /^users/, name: 'users' },
    { route: /^users\/(\w+)/, name: 'user' }
];

match();
//     match users
// Note that this probably isn't expected behavior
// if we look closely at the "uri". This illustrates
// the importance of order, when testing against a
// collection of URIs specs.

routes.reverse();

match();
//     match user
```

Logging initial configuration

Routers shouldn't start listening to URI change events until they're configured with all the relevant routes. For example, if individual components configure the router with the routes required by that component, we wouldn't want the router to start listening for URI change events until the component has a chance to configure its routes.

The main application component that initializes its subordinate components would probably bootstrap this process, and when completed, tell the router to start. When individual components have their own routes encapsulated within, it can be difficult, during development, to grasp the router configuration in its entirety. For this, we need an option in our router that will log its entire configuration—the patterns, and the events they trigger. This helps us scale because we don't have to sacrifice modular routes to get the big picture.

Logging route events

In addition to logging the initial route configuration, it's helpful if the router can log the lifecycle that takes place when a URI change event is triggered. This is different from the event mechanism logging that we discussed in the preceding chapter—these events will log after the router triggers a route event.

If we're building a large-scale JavaScript architecture with lots of routes, we'll want to know everything about our router, and how it behaves at runtime. The router is so fundamental to the scalability of our application that we'll want to invest in the minute details here.

For example, it can be useful to get an idea of what the router is doing as it's walking through the available routes, looking for a match. It's also useful to see the result of what's parsed out of the URI string by the router, so that we can compare that to what's seen by the route event handlers downstream. Not all router components will support this level of logging. If it turns out that we need it, some frameworks will provide sufficient entry points into their components, along with good extension mechanisms.

Handling invalid resource states

Sometimes, we forget that the router is stateless; it takes a URI string as input, and triggers events based on pattern-matching criteria. A scaling problem related to addressability isn't with the router state, but the state of components that listen to routes.

For example, imagine we navigate away from one resource to another. While we're visiting this new resource, a lot can happen with that first resource. Well, it's easy for it to change in ways that make it illegal for this particular user to visit, meanwhile, it's in their history and all they need to do is hit the back button.

It's edge cases like these that routers and addressability can introduce into our application. It's not, however, the responsibility of the router to handle these edge cases. They happen due to a combination of lots of URIs, lots of components, and complex business rules that tie them all together. The router is just a mechanism to help us cope with large-scale policies, not a place to implement policies.

Summary

This chapter went into detail on addressability, and how to achieve this architectural property as our application scales.

We began our discussion of routing and addressability with a look at the different approaches to routing—the hash change event and utilizing the history API available in modern browsers. Most frameworks abstract the differences away for us. Next, we looked at the responsibilities of routers, and how they should be decoupled from other components through triggering events.

The design of URIs themselves also plays a role in the scalability of our software, because they need to be consistent and predictable. Even the users can use this predictability to help themselves scale the use of our software. URIs encode information which is then relayed to our handlers that respond to routes; this also needs to be taken into consideration.

We then looked at the various ways in which routes are triggered. The standard approach here is to click a link. If our application is well connected, it's going to have links all over the place. To help us scale lots of links, we need a way to generate URI strings automatically. Next, we're going to look at the metadata our components need in order to function. These are the user preferences and default values for our components.

6
User Preferences and Defaults

Any sufficiently large JavaScript application needs to configure its components. The scope and nature of our component configuration varies on an application-by-application basis. There are a number of scaling factors that need to be considered when configuring our components, and we'll address these throughout the chapter.

We'll start of by identifying the types of preferences we'll have to deal with, and the remainder of the chapter will walk through specific scaling issues concerning these preferences and how to work around them.

Preference types

There're three main types of preferences we're concerned with when designing large-scale JavaScript architectures. These are locales, behavior, and appearance. In this section we'll provide a definition for each of the preference categories.

Locales

Applications today can't support just a single locale, if they're going to succeed on a global scale. Because of globalization and the internet, demand for applications created in another part of the world is the new norm. Therefore, we have to design our JavaScript architectures in a way that accommodates many locales, seamlessly. Users in one locale should be able to use our application with the same ease and confidence as users in any other locale.

The process of enabling components to use any locale is called
internationalization. Then, the process of creating locale-specific
data for our application is called **localization**.

What makes internationalization/localization so difficult is that it touches every visual
aspect of the user interface. This can amount to quite a lot, despite the fact that there
are many components that don't care about locales—like controllers or collections.
For example, any string labels that would otherwise be hard-coded in a template
somewhere, now need to pass through a locale-aware translation mechanism.

The language translations are hard enough on their own. But locale data consists of
anything and everything that's pertinent to a given culture that's using our software.
For example, the formats used for date/time or currency values. These are just the
most common and straightforward elements. Things can vary right down to how
quantities are measured, or right up to the layout of the entire page.

Behavior

Most behavioral aspects of our components reside in the code, and are unchanging.
Behavioral changes that happen in response to different preferences are subtle, yet
important. When there're many interacting components, there's bound to be an
incompatible combination that causes issues.

For example, a function found within the implementation of our component might get
a value it uses to compute something from a configuration value. This could be a user
preference, or it could be something we've put in place for the sake of maintainability.

Throughout the remainder of the chapter, we'll refer to individual
configuration values as preferences. We'll refer to the aggregate effect
of all preferences within a given component as configuration.

Behavioral preferences can have varied effects on what the user sees. A simple
example would be turning the component off, or, disabling it. This preference would
result in the component no longer rendering in the UI. Another preference would
determine how many elements are displayed. A common example here would be a
user telling the application how many search results they want to see per page.

These types of preferences don't always map directly to the end user. That is, a
component may have certain preferences that aren't directly exposed to the user.
It could be there for the sole purpose of developer flexibility, to reduce the amount
of code we write. Configurable components take many forms, and it's from this
perspective that we need to make sure we address them accordingly, to help scale
our software.

It's not just the frontend components we need to think about either, as a given preference may change backend behavior. This could be as simple as a query parameter preference, or another preference that results in a different API endpoint being used. All these seemingly innocuous preferences add up to far-reaching consequences, across the application, possibly impacting other users of the system.

Appearance

If a modern JavaScript application is going to scale across audience demographics, its appearance needs to be configurable. This requirement can range anywhere from a configurable logo, to interchangeable themes that have the potential to drastically alter the look and feel of the UI.

Generally speaking, changes in appearance are centered around CSS properties like fonts, colors, widths, border radiuses, and so on. While it's true that the majority of the CSS implementation isn't touched by the majority of JavaScript developers, we still need to be conscious of theme boundaries.

For instance, if we're flexible with our appearance and how it's configured, we may let our users select their own theme at runtime. So we'll need to implement a theme-switching mechanism with which the user interacts. Further, themed UIs mean that the preference will need to be stored and loaded somewhere.

So that's coarse-grained themes—what about fine-grained appearance configuration? The former is more prevalent however, configuring specific styles of individual components isn't out of the question. The appearance granularity level coincides with other scaling influencers, like where our software is deployed, and the capabilities of our configuration APIs.

Supporting locales

Having internationalization support throughout all our components is a good idea. In fact, there're a lot of JavaScript tools out there to aid with this task. Some are more stand-alone, and some are more tailored for specific frameworks. Using these tools is easy, but there's a lot more to localization that needs to be taken into consideration, especially in a scaling context.

Deciding on locales to support

Once we have software with internationalization support that's in production use, the next step is to decide which locales to support. When we go through the first step of ensuring that all our components are internationalized, we do so with just one locale — the default locale. And that's fine at first, it may be years before our first secondary locale support requirement.

This is generally what happens with newer software projects. We know that internationalization should be up there on our list of priorities, but it's easy to get sidetracked with everything else going on. The leading argument in favor of not spending effort on locale support is that it's not needed right away. The argument against this mindset is that internationalization is exceedingly difficult to implement after-the-fact, as our components grow. So it's yet another scale-related trade off to make. Do we want our application to scale across cultures, or is immediate time-to-market more important?

Exceptional cases aside, we'll assume that internationalization is a must-have — we need to prioritize which locales we'll support, versus those that can wait. For example, it's a bad idea to aim for mass locale support before it's actually required. Locales occupy physical space, and someone needs to maintain these locales. So without a customer to pay the cost of this added scaling complexity, it's not worthwhile.

Instead, the chosen locales should be based solely on customer demand. If we have hundreds of people looking for support in one locale, with less than a dozen people asking about another, the priority should be obvious. It can be helpful if we prioritize locale support the same as we would feature support.

Maintaining locales

First and foremost, if we support a given locale, we'll need to translate the string messages that are displayed throughout the UI. Some of these are statically coded in template files while other strings are found in our JavaScript modules. If only it were a matter of locating these strings, and translating them once. But rarely do strings stay the same forever — there are often subtle tweaks to be had. Also, as our software grows and more components are added, so too are strings to be translated.

The scaling factor for just string translations alone is the number of locales we support — which is why we need to be conscientiously supporting only a limited number of locales while we can get away with it. The complexity doesn't end there. For example, some message strings are straightforward to map from source language to target language. Things like grammar inflection — how words take on different meanings based modifications — aren't so straightforward. In fact, these usages sometimes require specialized use of the internationalization library.

Other localizable data, like date/time formats, don't require much maintenance. There're one or two formats used throughout the application for a given locale. For formats like these, customers will likely be happy with the standard format used for their culture. Luckily, there's **Common Locale Data Repository (CLDR)** data we can use in our projects—a downloadable repository of common locale data. This is a good starting point, because this data is good enough most of the time, and is easy to override upon request.

Setting the locale

Once we have our internationalization library in place, and a couple of locales, we can start testing how our application behaves from the perspective of different cultures. There are a number of items to consider for this behavior. For example, we need to facilitate the locale selection for the user and we need to keep track of that selection.

Choosing locales

There are two common approaches to locale selection in JavaScript applications. The first approach is using the `accept-language` request header. The second approach is a selector widget on a user settings page.

The nice thing about the `accept-language` approach is that there's no user input involved. Our application is sent to the user's browser preference for language, and from there, we can set the locale. The challenge is that this approach can be too restrictive from a usability perspective, and from an implementation perspective. For example, users may not have control over their browser language preferences, or the browser may not have preferences for locales our application supports.

 Another technical challenge with the `accept-language` request header approach is that there's no easy means to pass request headers from the browser to the JavaScript code—which is kind of insane since there're both in the browser! For example, if our JavaScript code needs to know the locale preference so it can load the appropriate locale data, it'll need access to the `accept-language` header. To do this, we need backend hacks.

The more flexible approach is to present the user with a locale selector widget, and from there, it's made explicit which locale the user would like activated. However, we'll need to figure out a way to store this locale selection so that the user doesn't have to repeatedly select their locale.

Storing locale preferences

The locale preference, once selected by the user, can be stored as a cookie value. The next time the application loads in the browser, we'll have the locale preference ready to go. Then we can mark the selector with the appropriate selection, as well as load the relevant locale data.

The problem with storing the locale preference in a cookie is that if the user moves to another browser, the same selection process will need to be repeated. This can be a real problem these days as users are more mobile than ever—changes made on one device should be reflected anywhere the application is used. And that's just not possible with cookies.

If we use a backend API to store the locale preference, it'll be available everywhere for the user. The next challenge is loading the relevant locale data so that it's available for the rest of our components to use. Generally, we want this data ready before we start rendering data, so it's one of the first requests we'll make to the backend. Sometimes, all locales are served together, as one resource. This can be a problem if we support lots of locales, because of the up-front cost to load it.

On the other hand, once we load the locale preference, we can load only the immediately required locale. This will boost the initial load-time, but the trade-off is that it's slower to switch to a new locale. This is unlikely to happen often, so it's probably best to not load locale data that's never used.

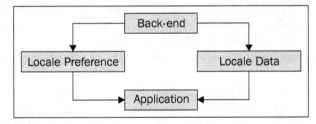

The JavaScript application first loads the locale preference, then uses that to load the local data

Locales in URIs

In addition to storing the local preference in the backend or as a cookie value, locales can be encoded as part of the URI. Often, they're expressed as a two character code—such as en or fr—and found at the beginning of the URI. The advantage of using this approach is that there's no storage required for the preference. We'd still likely want a selector for the user to choose their preferred locale, but this would result in a new URI instead of a preference value being stored somewhere.

Encoding the preferred locale in URIs like this has the same drawbacks as the cookie-based approach. While we can bookmark a URI, or pass a URI along to someone else—they'll see the same locale we do—the problem is that this isn't a permanent preference. Mind you, we could always store the preference and update the URI when the application is loaded. But this won't scale well due to the added complexities around routing and URI generation.

Generic component configuration

As we saw in the preceding section on locale preferences, we need to load a preference value, which can then be used by each of our components. Or maybe just one component in the case of locales, but this preference value indirectly impacts all components. Looking beyond locales, there're a lot of other things we'll want to configure in our components. This section looks at the problem from a generic perspective. First we need to decide on which aspects of a given component are configurable, and then there are the mechanics of getting those preferences into the components at runtime.

Deciding on configuration values

The first step with component configuration is deciding on preferences—which aspects of the component need to be configurable, and which aspects can stay static? It's far from an exact science, as more often than not, we realize later on that something static should have been configurable. Trial and error is the best process for finding configurable preferences, especially as our software is just getting off the ground. Too much initial configurability deliberation is a scaling bottleneck.

When something isn't configurable, it has the advantage of simplicity. It's more structural, and less of a moving part. This removes potential edge cases and performance issues. Up-front justification for making the value configurable doesn't happen all that often. As our software matures though, we'll have a better perspective, having put some preferences in place, and we'll have a better idea of what to expect.

For instance, we'll start seeing duplication across several of our components. They'll be largely the same, with only subtle variations. If we keep adding new types of components that differ minutely from one another, we're in for scaling trouble. Our code base will grow to an unmanageable size, and we'll confuse developers because the responsibilities of a given component will be blurred.

This is where we leverage configurability to achieve scale. This is done by introducing preferences in favor of new component types. For example, say we need a new view that is identical to another view that's used in several places already, aside from the way it handles a DOM event. Rather than implement a new view type, we would enhance the existing view, to accept a new function value that overrides the default for this event.

On the flipside, we can't just go introducing component preferences willy-nilly. When we do that, we replace old scaling bottlenecks with new ones. There's performance to take into consideration, because it takes a hit with every new configurable preference we add. There's the code complexity — it's not as straightforward to use preferences as it is static values. There's the possibility of introducing preferences that are inconsistent with other preferences introduced during the same development cycle by other developers. Finally, there's the matter of keeping track and documenting all the various preferences available to a given component.

Stored and hard-coded default values

As far as components are concerned, preferences should be treated as closely to regular JavaScript variables as possible. This keeps our code flexible — replacing a preference with a static value shouldn't have a big impact. Regular variables are usually declared with an initial value, and preferences should be declared with a default value as well. That way, if we can't get at the preference that's stored in the backend for some reason, the software will continue to function using a sane default value.

There should always be a fallback default value for any preference, and these values should be documented somewhere. Ideally the default values used serve the common case, so not every preference needs to be tinkered with just in order to use the software. If for some reason we can't access the stored configuration values from the backend, the hard-coded default values keep the software running, albeit, using a less than ideal configuration.

 Sometimes, not having access to the configuration values is a non-starter and the software should fail-fast instead of using the hard-coded default values. While the software is fully-functional using the defaults, depending on our customers and their deployment, this mode may be worse than the software being unavailable. Something to consider when deploying large-scale JavaScript applications.

Default preference values make it safe to delete modified preference values in the backend. Think of it as a reset to the factory settings action. In other words, if we introduce problems into the software by adjusting preference values, we can just remove our stored values. If there's no need to store default values in the backend, then there's no risk of overriding the defaults.

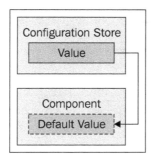

Defaults are always there, but can easily be overridden by preference values from the backend

Backend implications

If we're storing our preference values in the backend to provide portability for our users, then we need some mechanism that allows us to put new value preferences in the configuration store, as well as retrieve our preferences. Ideally, this would be an API that lets us define arbitrary key-value preferences, and lets us retrieve all our configuration with one request.

The reason this is so valuable to frontend development is that we can define new preferences for our components as we develop them, without being disruptive to the backend team. As far as the backend API is concerned, frontend configuration is arbitrary—the API works the same with or without a UI.

Sometimes, this can actually be more of a headache than it's worth. What if there's very little variation—only a handful of configuration values required throughout the application? If that's the case, we might consider maintaining a static JSON file that serves as our frontend configuration. It's arbitrary enough that we can define preferences ad-hoc, and it works the same as an API, as far as fetching the preference values goes.

Where this doesn't work so well is when there are user-defined preferences. For example, the user's preferred locale. Our application might have a default locale specified, until the user changes it. They're changing the preference for themselves, not every user in the system. This is where we need the aforementioned configuration API. The way it stores these values, in a database most likely, needs to be user-sensitive. This isn't true of every preference value though; some are set by the deployment operators and users can't touch these.

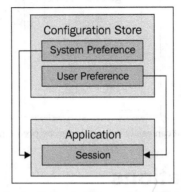

The current user session can be used to load preferences specific to that user; these are different from system settings, which don't vary by user

Loading configuration values

There're two approaches to loading configuration required by the frontend. The first approach is to load all configuration because anything is rendered in the UI. This means that before the router starts to process anything, we would wait for the configuration to be available. This generally means waiting on a promise that loads the configuration data. The obvious downside here is that the initial load time suffers. The upside is that we have everything we need going forward—no more configuration requests.

We can use local storage in the browser to cache preference values. They seldom change, and this tactic has the potential to boost initial-load performance. On the other hand, it adds complexity—so only consider this if there're a lot of configuration values and the time taken to load them is noticeable.

Instead of loading all our configuration up-front, preference values can be loaded on demand. That is, when a component is about to be instantiated, a request is made for its configuration. This has the appeal of being efficient, but again, how much configuration could there possibly be to warrant such complexity? Strive toward loading all application configuration up-front where possible.

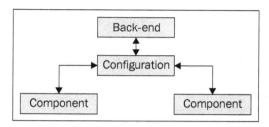

A configuration component that communicates with the backend provides an abstraction for any components that get or set preference values

Configuring behavior

The behavior of our components is largely self-contained, if implemented well. What they expose to the outside world are preferences that make subtle adjustments to their behavior. This could be something that's internally-focused — such as the type of model that's used, or the preferred algorithm. It could be something that's user-facing, such as enabling components, or setting display modes. It's these preferences that help us scale our components to work in a variety of contexts.

Enabling and disabling components

Once our software reaches a certain critical mass, not all features will be relevant to all users. The simple ability to toggle components between an enabled/disabled state is a powerful tool. Both for us, as a software vendor, and for our customers. For example, we know that some features are required by certain user roles in our software, but they're not the common case. To better optimize for the common user, we may choose to disable certain advanced features that aren't used as often. This can clean up the layout, improve performance, and so on.

On the other hand, we may have all our features turned on by default, but if components have the ability to be turned off, then that lets the user decide what's relevant to them. If they can arrange the UI to their liking, removing elements that are of no particular use to them, then it makes for a better user experience.

In either case, there're implications as far as the layout as a whole is concerned. If we don't take the time to design our layouts in a scalable way, then toggling components really doesn't add any value. During the design of our layout, we need to walk through the various configuration scenarios that the user might use, or that we ourselves might use.

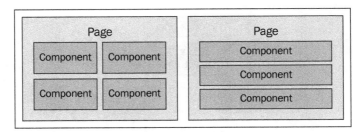

Disabling components on a page has the potential to update the layout; our styles need to by able to handle this

Changing quantities

The quantity of something displayed in the UI is something that's at best a guess made at design time. We hope that the number of items displayed in a list is the optimal number, and the user doesn't have to fuss with changing these types of preferences. The problem is that quantities are very subjective. It's more about the individual that's using our application to perform a task, and depending on what they're used to, what they're doing in conjunction with using our software, and a host of other factors, the quantity preference default may not be optimal.

A common quantity question is how many entities do I want displayed on my screen? The entities can be common grid widgets that're used throughout the application, a search results page, or anything else that renders a collection of things. We can opt for the efficient default of a smaller quantity to display, while allowing for larger quantities that suit the user's needs.

It's always a good idea to sanity-check the user provided preferences. One safeguard is to put a selection of allowable values in place, rather than accepting arbitrary user input. We shouldn't allow for 1,000 entities to be rendered in a grid, for instance. Although, the API that returns this data should sanity-check and cap quantity arguments as well.

Another quantity consideration is which entity properties do we need displayed? In the case of grids, we may want to see certain columns while hiding others. Something like this is a preference that ought to be persistent, because if we go through the effort of setting up the data we want to see, we won't want to repeat that effort.

When we change quantity preferences, there're backend implications. In the case of how many entities to render, we probably want to pass this constraint along to the API when we're fetching the data—there's no point in fetching something we're not going to display. There may be model or collection implications as well. In the case of figuring out which data we want displayed in a particular UI region, we might ask the model or collection for only a subset of what they have.

Changing order

The order in which a collection is rendered in the UI is another common behavioral preference, one that we'll most likely want to support. The biggest impact here is configuring the default order of something. For example, ordering every collection by the modified date, so that the most recent entities appear first, is a good default.

Many grid components will let the user toggle the ordering of a given column between ascending and descending. These are actions, not necessarily preferences. However, they can grow to be annoying actions if the default order is never what we want. So we may want to introduce a means for the user to provide a default ordering preference for any given grid, while retaining the ability click column headers to sort ad-hoc.

More complex ordering preferences are possible, and clickable column headers don't always help here. For instance, what if we want to order by something that's not actually rendered in the UI, like relevance or best selling? There's probably a control we can use for this, but it's another potential preference—since it could help provide a better experience.

```js
// users.js
export default class Users {

    // Accepts a "collection" array, and an "order"
    // string.
    constructor(collection, order) {
        this.collection = collection;
        this.order = order;

        // Creates an iterator so we can iterate over
```

```javascript
            // the "collection" array without having to
            // directly access it.
            this[Symbol.iterator] = function*() {
                for (let user of this.collection) {
                    yield user;
                }
            };
        }

    set order(order) {

            // When the order break it down into it's parts,
            // the "key" and the "direction".
            var [ key, direction ] = order.split(' ');

            // Sorts the collection. If the property value can be
            // converted to lower case, they it's converted to avoid
            // case inconsistencies.
            this.collection.sort((a, b) => {
                var aValue = typeof a[key].toLowerCase === 'function' ?
                    a[key].toLowerCase() : a[key];

                var bValue = typeof b[key].toLowerCase === 'function' ?
                    b[key].toLowerCase() : b[key];

                if (aValue < bValue) {
                    return -1;
                } else if (aValue > bValue) {
                    return 1;
                } else {
                    return 0;
                }
            });

            // If the direction is "desc", we need to reverse the sort.
            if (direction === 'desc') {
                this.collection.reverse();
            }
        }

}

// main.js
```

```
import Users from 'users.js';

var users = new Users([
    { name: 'Albert' },
    { name: 'Craig' },
    { name: 'Beth' }
], 'name');

console.log('Ascending order...');
for (let user of users) {
    console.log(user.name);
}
//
// Albert
// Beth
// Craig

users.order = 'name desc';

console.log('Descending order...');
for (let user of users) {
    console.log(user.name);
}
//
// Craig
// Beth
// Albert
```

Configuring notifications

When users perform some action in our application, like turning something on or off, we need to provide feedback on the state of that action. Did it succeed? Did it fail? Is it running? These are generally done through notifications, rendered as transient popups in the corner of the screen, or in a panel somewhere.

The user may want to control certain aspects about how they're notified—there's nothing more irritating than getting spammed with information we don't care about. So one preference related to notifications might be a selection of notification topics. For example, we might want to opt out of notifications for irrelevant entity types.

Another potential preference might be the duration that a given notification stays active on the screen. For example, should it stay where it is till we acknowledge it, or should it go away after three seconds? In the extreme case, the user may want to turn off notifications altogether if there's no other way to make them less annoying. There are always the action logs for convenient browsing later on if need be.

Inline options

How do we collect user preference input? For the less active, global application preferences, a settings page divided into categories probably makes sense. However, having to configure things specific to individual widgets on a settings page is kind of annoying. It's sometimes better to have inline options.

Inline means that the user can set their preference using elements that are part of the UI in question. For example, choosing specific columns to display in a grid. It wouldn't make much sense to bury such a preference in a settings page somewhere. When preference controls are positioned relative to the thing they control, it requires less explanation. The user can generally figure out the meaning a lot easier when the control is contextual.

 The downside to contextual preference controls is that they have potential to clutter the UI. If there're a lot of components on the page, each of which has preferences controls on it, then we're most likely creating confusion instead of convenience.

Changing the look and feel

Today, it's less common for the look and feel of an application to be a static, unchanging aspect. Instead, they ship with a handful of themes the user can choose from. Or, the support to easily create themes is built into the software. This allows our customers to decide how our software should look for their users. In addition to packaged themes that update the look and feel of our application, individual style preferences may be set.

Theme tools

If we want our application to have the ability to change themes upon request, we have to put a lot of design and architecture into our CSS and the markup that uses it. While this topic goes way beyond the scope of this book, it's worth looking at the tools available for assisting in generating themes.

The first tool at our disposal in this area is a CSS framework. Like JavaScript frameworks, CSS frameworks define consistent patterns and conventions. It's then up to us, the component authors, to figure out how to apply these CSS patterns to our components, and the markup they generate. Think of a theme as a bunch of style preferences. When the configuration is changed, the appearance is changed because of new preference values. What makes a CSS module a theme, is having the same properties defined as all the other themes used by the application—it's only the values of these properties that change.

Another tool we can use is part of the backend build process—CSS compilers. These tools take in files that use a dialect of CSS, and preprocess them. What's nice about these types of preprocessor languages is that we have much greater control of how style preferences are specified. For example, there's no such thing as variables in CSS, but preprocessors have them, and this is a really handy configurability feature to have.

Selecting a theme

Once we have a theme-able user interface, we need a way to load a specific theme instance. Even if we don't allow users to select a theme of their choice, it's still nice to be able to change the design by changing a preference value. When we decide to implement a new design, this certainly makes deployment into a production environment that much simpler.

Down the road, we may decide that we do want to let users select their own theme. For example, we might have acquired lots of users and there's now a demand for this ability. We can create the theme selector like any other preference value that's used in the system. We'd need to have some kind of theme selection widget in place, and the selection made by the user can map to a path, since this is likely all that's needed to swap one theme for another.

Another possibility is to have different themes set as the default, based on the role of the user. For example, if an administrator logs in, it's helpful to have a different visual cue that you are in fact logged in as a specific type of user. This type of thing can help in scenarios where there're screenshots, and so on.

Individual style preferences

The look and feel of an application can change at an individual element level. That is, if we want to change the width of something, we can change it on the screen. Or maybe we don't like the font face that's in use and we want to change that as well, but nothing else.

These types of fine-grained style preferences should be avoided because they do not scale well. Our components have to be aware of specific style considerations, and that degrades the true purpose of the component in most cases. In some cases, picking a different layout for a screen doesn't hurt, because that usually means swapping one CSS class for another.

Another possibility is using drag and drop interactions to set the size of something. But, it's best if these are kept as transient interactions, and not as persistent preferences. We want to optimize for the common configuration values, and there's nothing common about the resizing of elements to individual tastes.

Performance implications

We'll close the chapter out with an overview of the performance implications introduced by the various configuration areas discussed thus far. If we really need configuration values in one area because they add value, they may hurt performance overall—so we need to offset this cost somehow.

Configurable locale performance

By far the most noticeable performance bottleneck concerning locales is the initial load. That's because we have to load all the locale data before anything is actually rendered for the user. This includes string message translations, as well as all the other data necessary for localization. The performance during initialization is constrained further when there's more than one locale loaded up-front.

The best way to improve the load performance is to only load the locale that the user actually wants. Once they've set this preference, they're unlikely to change it frequently, so there's no real benefit to having other locale data nearby and ready.

There's an unavoidable slow-down in rendering views, because much data needs to pass through the localization mechanism we're using. This alone isn't likely to cause performance issues because most operations are small and efficient—simple lookups, and string formatting. The additional overhead is there though, and needs to be accounted for.

Configurable behavior performance

Configuration that alters the behavior of a component also has minimal performance impact. In fact, the performance characteristics of configurable behavior are similar to those of configurable locales. The biggest challenge is the initial configuration load. After that, it's just a matter of performing lookups, which are fast.

The thing to look out for, is when we have lots of components we need to configure. While individual lookups are fast, performance takes a hit when there're lots of lookups. It'll take quite a while to reach this point, but the risk is there nonetheless.

The following is an example that shows how we can configure when a collection is sorted, impacting the performance of other operations that are order-dependent and are called frequently:

```js
// users.js
export default class Users {

    // The users collection excepts data, and an
    // "order" property name.
    constructor(collection, order) {
        this.collection = collection;
        this.order = order;
        this.ordered = !!order;
    }

    // Whenever the "order" property is set, we need
    // to sort the internal "collection" array.
    set order(key) {
        this.collection.sort((a, b) => {
            if (a[key] < b[key]) {
                return -1;
            } else if (a[key] > b[key]) {
                return 1;
            } else {
                return 0;
            }
        });
    }

    // Finds the smallest item of the collection. If the
    // collection is ordered, then we can just return the
    // first collection item. Otherwise, we need to iterate
    // over the collection to find the smallest item.
    min(key) {
        if (this.ordered) {
            return this.collection[0];
        } else {
            var result = {};
            result[key] = Number.POSITIVE_INFINITY;

            for (let item of this.collection) {
```

```javascript
                    if (item[key] < result[key]) {
                        result = item;
                    }
                }

                return result;
            }
        }

        // The inverse of the "min()" function, returns the
        // last collection item if ordered. Otherwise, it looks
        // for the largest item.
        max(key) {
            if (this.ordered) {
                return this.collection[this.collection.length - 1];
            } else {
                var result = {};
                result[key] = Number.NEGATIVE_INFINITY;

                for (let item of this.collection) {
                    if (item[key] > result[key]) {
                        result = item;
                    }
                }

                return result;
            }
        }

}

// main.js
import Users from 'users.js';

var users;

// Creates an "ordered" users collection.
users = new Users([
    { age: 23 },
    { age: 19 },
    { age: 51 },
    { age: 39 }
], 'age');

// Calling "min()" and "max()" doesn't result in
```

```
// two iterations over the collection because they're
// already ordered.
console.log('ordered min', users.min());
console.log('ordered max', users.max());
//
// ordered min {age: 19}
// ordered max {age: 51}

// Creates an "unordered" users collection.
users = new Users([
    { age: 23 },
    { age: 19 },
    { age: 51 },
    { age: 39 }
]);

// Every time "min()" or "max()" is called, we
// have to iterate over the collection to find
// the smallest or largest item.
console.log('unordered min', users.min('age'));
console.log('unordered max', users.max('age'));
//
// unordered min {age: 19}
// unordered max {age: 51}
```

Behavioral preferences may be used to completely swap one function for another. They may have the same interface, but with different implementations. Deciding which function to use at runtime isn't expensive, but there's also the memory consumption to consider. For example, if there're many preferences throughout our application that support different functions, we'll have to store the default implementation, in addition to the function stored as a preference value.

Configurable theme performance

The only real latency we can expect from configurable themes is the initial cost of figuring out which theme to use. Then there's the process of downloading it, and applying the styles to the markup—which isn't any different from an application with a single set of static styles. If we allow the user to switch themes, there's the additional latency of waiting for the new CSS and related static resources to download and render.

Summary

This chapter introduced the concept of configurability in large-scale JavaScript applications. The major configuration categories are locales, behavior, and appearance. Locales are a big part of web applications today because there's nothing stopping people, anywhere in the world, from using our application. There are scaling challenges associated with internationalization though. It adds complexity to our development lifecycle and there's the cost of maintaining locales.

Preferences need to be stored somewhere. Storing them in the browser works, but there's no portability with this approach. It's much more appropriate to store preferences in the backend and load them when the application initializes. There're many challenges to scaling lots of preferences, including differentiating between user-defined and system preferences. It shouldn't matter if we've included sane hard-coded default values.

The styles of our application are another configurable dimension. There're frameworks and build-tools that help us build themes for the look and feel. Configurable components have minor performance considerations—the next chapter will look at performance challenges that crop up as we scale our software.

7
Load Time and Responsiveness

JavaScript scalability includes the *load time* of the application, and the *responsiveness* of the application when the user interacts with it. Collectively, we refer to these two architectural qualities as performance. Performance is the prominent indicator of quality in the eyes of a user — it's important to get it right.

As our applications acquire new features and as the user base grows, we must find a way to avoid the associated performance degradation. The initial load is affected by things such as the JavaScript artifact payload size. The responsiveness of our UI has more to do with the runtime characteristics of our code.

Throughout this chapter, we'll address these two dimensions of performance, and how the various trade-offs we'll make will impact other areas of the system.

Component artifacts

Earlier on in the book, we had emphasized that large-scale JavaScript applications are just collections of components. These components communicate with one another in complex and intricate ways — these communications are what realize the behavior of our system. Before components can communicate, they have to be delivered to the browser. It's helpful in understanding what these components are made of, and how they're actually delivered to the browser. Then we can reason about the initial load time of our application.

Component dependencies

Components are the bedrocks of our application; that means we need to deliver them to the browser, and execute them in some coherent manner. The components themselves can range from being monolithic JavaScript files, to something that's spread out over several modules. All the puzzle pieces are put together through the dependency graph. We start off with an application component, as this is the entry point into our application. It finds all the components it needs by requiring them. For example, there may only be a handful of top-level components, which map to the key features of our software. This is the first level of the dependency tree, and unless all our feature components are composed monolithically, there'll probably further module dependencies to resolve.

The module loading mechanism progresses through the tree until it has everything it needs. What's nice about modules and dependencies, broken down to a reasonable level of granularity, is that a lot of complexity is masked. We don't have to hold the entire dependency graph in our heads, an unreasonable goal for even medium-scale applications.

With this modular structure, and the mechanism used to load and process dependencies, comes performance implications. Namely, the initial load time is impacted since the module loader needs to walk through the dependency graph, and ask the backend for each resource. While the requests are asynchronous, the network overhead exists nonetheless — that's what hurts us the most during the initial load.

However, just because we want a modular structure, doesn't mean we have to suffer the consequences of network overhead. Especially as we start scaling to lots of features and lots of users. There's more to deliver to each client session, and there's more resource contention in the backend as more users ask for the same thing. Module dependencies are traceable, which give our build tools a number of options.

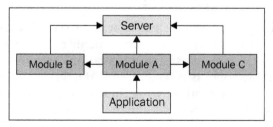

How JavaScript application modules are loaded; dependencies are automatically loaded

Building components

When our components reach a certain level of complexity, they'll likely require more than just a few modules to realize all their functionality. Multiply this by a growing number of components, and we've got ourselves a network request overhead issue. Even if the modules carry a small payload, there's still the network overhead to consider.

We should actually strive for smaller modules, as they're more easily consumed by other developers—if they're small, they likely have less moving parts. As we saw in the preceding section, modules and the dependencies amongst them, enable us to divide and conquer. That's because the module loader traces the dependency graph and pulls in the modules as they're needed.

If we want to avoid hitting the backend with so many requests, we can build larger component artifacts as part of our build toolchain. There are many tools out there, that directly leverage the module loader to trace the dependencies, and build the corresponding components, like RequireJS and Browserify. This is important because it means that we can choose a level of module granularity that suits our application, and still be able to build larger component artifacts. Or we can switch back to loading smaller modules into the browser on the fly.

The scaling implications in terms of network request overhead make big difference. The more components, and the larger these components are, the more this build process matters. Especially since uglification, the process of shrinking down the file size, is often part of the process. Being able to turn these build steps off, on the other hand, has scaling implications for the development team as well. If we can switch back and forth between the types of component artifacts delivered to the browser, the development process can move forward much quicker.

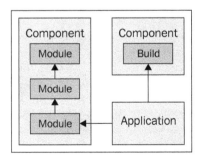

Building components results in fewer requested artifacts, and fewer network requests

Loading components

In this section, we'll take a look at the mechanisms responsible for actually loading our source modules and built components into the browser. There are many third-party tools in use today for structuring our modules and declaring their dependencies, but the trend is moving toward using newer browser standards for these tasks. We'll also look at lazily loading our modules, and the usability implications for load latency.

Loading modules

Many large-scale applications in production today use technologies such as RequireJS and Browserify. RequireJS is a pure JavaScript module loader and has tools that can build larger components. The aim with Browserify is to build components that run in the browser, using code that was written for Node.js. While both these technologies solve many of the issues discussed so far in this chapter, the new ECMAScript 6 module approach is the way forward.

The main argument in favor of using the browser-based approach to module loading and dependency management is that there's no longer a need for another third-party tool. If the language has a feature to solve a scaling issue, it's always better to go that route, because there's less work for us. It's certainly not a silver bullet, but it does have a lot of the functionality we require.

For example, we no longer have to rely on sending Ajax requests, and evaluating the JavaScript code when it arrives—that's all up to the browser now. The syntax itself is actually more aligned with the standard `import export` keywords found in other programming languages. On the other hand, native JavaScript modules are still new hotness, and that's not really justification enough to throw away code that's using a different module loader. For new projects, it's worth looking at ES6 transpiler technologies that allow us to start using these new module constructs from the start.

A portion of the network overhead our application experiences, and the user ultimately pays for, has to do with the HTTP specification. The latest draft Version of the spec, 2.0, addresses a lot of overhead and performance issues. What does this mean for loading modules? Well, if we can get reasonable network performance with minimal overhead, we might be able to simplify our artifacts. The need to compile larger components can be de-prioritized in favor of focusing on a solid modular architecture.

Lazy module loading

One advantage we lose with monolithically compiled components is the opportunity to defer loading of certain modules till they're actually required. With compiled components, it's all or nothing—which is especially true if our entire frontend is compiled into a single JavaScript artifact. On the plus side, everything is there when it's needed. If the user decides to interact with a feature five minutes after the initial load, the code is already in the browser, ready to go.

Lazy loading, on the other hand, is the default mode. This simply means that the module isn't loaded into the browser till some other component explicitly asks for it. This could mean either a `require()` call or an `import` statement. Until these calls are made, they're not fetched from the backend. The advantage being, the initial page load should be a lot faster, it's only pulling in the modules it needs for the features displayed to the user initially.

On the other hand, when the user goes to use some feature, five minutes after the initial load, our application will be requiring or importing some modules for the first time. This means that there's some latency involved after the initial load. Mind you, the modules that are loaded on demand, later on in the session, should be small in number. Because there're bound to be some shared modules loaded up-front by the initial page presented to the user.

We have to put some thought into the dependencies throughout our system. While we may think we're deferring the loading of certain modules, there could be some indirect dependencies that inadvertently load modules for the home screen, when they're not actually needed. The network panel in the developer tools is ideal for this, as it's usually obvious that we're loading things we don't actually need. If our application has lots of features, lazy loading is especially helpful. The savings on initial load time are big, and there are likely to be features that the user never uses, and hence never needs to load.

Next is an example that shows the concept of not loading modules until they're actually needed:

```
// stuff.js
// Export something we can call from another module...
export default function doStuff() {
    console.log('doing stuff');
}


// main.js
// Don't import "doStuff()" till the link
```

```
// is clicked.
document.getElementById('do-link')
    .addEventListener('click', function(e) {
        e.preventDefault();

        // In ES6, it's just "System.import()" - which isn't easy
        // to do across environments yet.
        var loader = new traceur.runtime.BrowserTraceurLoader();
        loader.import('stuff.js').then(function(stuff) {
            stuff.default();
        });
    });
```

Module load latency

Modules load in response to events, and these are almost always user events. The application is launched. A tab is selected. These types of events have the potential to load new modules if they haven't been loaded already. The challenge is what can we do for the user while these code modules are in transit, or being evaluated? Because it's the code we're waiting on, we can't exactly execute code that makes for a better loading experience.

For example, until we have a module loaded, and until all its dependencies have been loaded, we can't do things that are critical to the user-perceived responsiveness of our UI. These are things like making API calls, and manipulating the DOM to provide user feedback. Without data from the API, all we can tell the user is, *sit tight, stuff is loading!* If the user is frustrated enough, because our modules are taking a while and the loading indicator isn't going away, they'll start randomly clicking elements that look clickable. If we don't have any event handlers setup for these, then the UI will feel unresponsive.

'Following is an example that shows how an imported module that runs expensive code, can block code in the importing module from running:

```
// delay.js

var i = 10000000;

// Eat some CPU cycles, causing a delay in any
// modules that import this one.
console.log('delay', 'active');
while (i--) {
```

```
    for (let c = 0; c < 1000; c++) {

    }
}
console.log('delay', 'complete');

// main.js

// Importing this module will block, because
// it runs some expensive code.
import 'delay.js';

// The link is displayed, and it looks clickable,
// but nothing happens. Because there's no event
// handler setup yet.
document.getElementById('do-link')
    .addEventListener('click', function(e) {
        e.preventDefault();
        console.log('clicked');
    });
```

Networks aren't predictable, nor are the scaling influencers our application is facing in the backend. Lot's of users means there's a potential for high latency with loading our modules. We have to account for these circumstances if we want to scale. This involves the use of tactics. The first module we need to load, after the main application, is something that's capable of notifying the user.

For example, our UI has a default loader element, but when our first module loads, it proceeds to render more detailed information on what's loading and how long it might take, or, it just might have to deliver the bad news that there's something wrong with the network or the backend. As we scale, these types of unpleasant events will happen. If we want to keep scaling up, we have to account for them early on, and make the UI always feel responsive, even when it isn't.

Communication bottlenecks

When our application acquires more moving parts, it acquires more communication overhead. That's because our components need to communicate with one another in order to realize the larger behavior of our features. We could reduce the inter-component communication overhead to essentially zero, if we were so inclined, but then we would face the issue of monolithic and repetitive code. If we want modular components, communication has to happen, but that comes at a cost.

This section looks at some issues we'll face as we scale our software in terms of communication bottlenecks. We need to look for the trade-offs that improve communication performance, without sacrificing modularity. One of the most effective ways to do that is by using the profiling tools available in our web browsers. They can reveal the same responsiveness issues that the user experiences while interacting with our UI.

Reducing indirection

The primary abstraction, by which our components communicate with one another, is an event broker. It's the job of the broker to maintain the list of subscribers for any given event type. Our JavaScript applications scale in two respects—the number of subscribers for a given event type, and the number of event types. In terms of performance bottlenecks, this can get out of control quickly.

The first thing we'll want to pay close attention to is the composition of our features. To implement a feature, we'll follow the same pattern of existing features. This means that we'll use the same component types, the same events, and so on. There are subtle variations, but the over-arching pattern is the same across features. This is a good practice: following the same pattern from feature to feature. The patterns used are a good starting point to figure out how to reduce overhead.

For example, say the pattern we're using throughout our application requires 8-10 components to realize a given feature. That's too much overhead. Any one of these components communicates with several others, and some of the abstractions just aren't all that valuable. They looked good in our heads and on paper, as we designed the architecture where the pattern originated. Now that we've implemented the pattern, that initial value has diluted a bit, and is now a performance issue.

Next is an example that shows how simply adding new components is enough to increase communication overhead costs exponentially:

```
// component.js
import events from 'events.js';

// A generic component...
export default class Component {

    // When created, this component triggers an
    // event. It also adds a listener for that
    // same event, and does some expensive work.
    constructor() {
        events.trigger('CreateComponent');
```

```
        events.listen('CreateComponent', () => {
            var i = 100000;
            while (--i) {
                for (let c = 0; c < 100; c++) {}
            }
        });
    }
};

// main.js
import Component from 'component.js';

// A place to hold our created components...
var components = [];

// Any time the add button is clicked, a new
// component is created. As more and more components
// are added, we can see a noticeable impact on
// the overall latency of the system.
// Click this button for long enough, and the browser
// tab crashes.
document.getElementById('add')
    .addEventListener('click', function() {
        console.clear();
        console.time('event overhead');
        components.push(new Component());
        console.timeEnd('event overhead');
        console.log('components', components.length);
    });
```

Loosely coupled components are a good thing, as they separate concerns, and give us more implementation freedoms with less risk of breaking other components. The way we couple our components establishes a repeatable pattern. At some point after initial implementation, as our software matures, we will realize that the pattern that once served us well is now too heavy. The concerns of our components are well understood, and we have no need for the implementation freedoms we thought we might need. The solution to this is changing the pattern. The pattern is what's followed, so it's the ultimate indicator of what our code will look like in future components. It's the best place to fix communication bottlenecks, by removing unnecessary components.

Profiling code

We can get an intuitive sense, just by looking at our code; that there's a lot more going on than there needs to be. As we saw in the preceding section, the inter-component communication patterns we use throughout the application are quite telling. We can see the excessive components at a logical design level, but what about the physical level during runtime?

Before we go and start re-factoring our code, changing patterns, removing components, and so on, we need to profile our code. This will give us an idea of the runtime performance characteristics of our code, and not just how it appears. Profiles give us the information we need to make useful decisions on optimizations. Most importantly, by profiling our code, we can avoid micro-optimizations that have little or no impact on the end user's experience. At the very least, we can prioritize the performance issues we need to tackle. Communication overhead between our components is likely to take top priority, as it has the most tangible impact on the user, and is a huge scaling obstacle.

The first tool available to us is the built-in profiling tools of the browser. We can manually use the developer tools UI to profile the entire application as we interact with it. This is useful for diagnosing specific responsiveness issues in the UI. We can also write code that uses the same in-browser profiling mechanism to target smaller pieces of code, like individual functions, and get the same output. The resulting profile is essentially a call stack, with a breakdown of how much CPU time is spent where. This points us in the right direction, so we can focus our efforts on optimizing expensive code.

 We're only scratching the surface of profiling JavaScript application performance. This is a huge topic, and you can Google "Profiling JavaScript code" — there are a ton of good resources out there. Here's a great resource to get you started: https://developer.chrome.com/devtools/docs/cpu-profiling

Next is an example that shows how to use the browser developer tools to create a profile that compares several functions:

```
// Eat some CPU cycles, and call other functions
// to establish a profilable call stack...
function whileLoop() {
    var i = 100000;

    while (--i) {
```

```
            forLoop1(i);
            forLoop2(i);
        }
    }

// Eat some CPU cycles...
function forLoop1(max) {
    for (var i = 0; i < max; i++) {
        i * i;
    }
}

// Eat less CPU cycles...
function forLoop2(max) {
    max /= 2;
    for (var i = 0; i < max; i ++) {
        i * i;
    }
}

// Creates the profile in the "profile" tab
// of dev tools.
console.profile('main');
whileLoop();
console.profileEnd('main');
// 1177.9ms 1.73% forLoop1
// 1343.2ms 1.98% forLoop2
```

Other tools that profile JavaScript code exist outside of the browser. We use these for different purposes. For example, benchmark.js and tools similar to it, are used to measure the raw performance of our code. The output tells us how many operations per second our code is running at. The really useful aspect of this approach is comparing two or more function implementations. The profile can give as a breakdown of which function is the fastest, and by what margin. At the end of the day, that's the most important profiling information we need.

Component optimization

Now that we've fixed our component communication performance bottlenecks, it's time to look inside our components, at the implementation specifics and the performance issues they may present. For example, maintaining state is a common requirement of JavaScript components, however, this does not scale well performance-wise because of all the book-keeping code required. We also need to be aware of side effects introduced by functions that mutate data that other components use. Finally, the DOM itself, and the way our code interacts with it, has much potential for unresponsiveness.

Components that maintain state

Most components in our code need to maintain state, and this is unavoidable for the most part. For example, if our component is composed of a model and a view, the view needs to know when to render itself, based on the state of the model. The view also holds a reference to a DOM element—either directly or through a selector string—and any given element has state, at all times.

So state is a fact of life in our components—what's the big deal? There isn't one, really. In fact, we get to write some really nice event-driven code that reacts to these changes in state, resulting in a change to what the user is looking at. The problem comes when we scale, of course; our components, on an individual basis, acquire more state to maintain, our data model served up by the backend grows more complex, and the DOM elements grow as well. All these things with state depend on one another. There's a multitude of complexity as systems like these grow, and can really hurt performance.

Thankfully, the frameworks we use, handle a lot of this complexity for us. Not only that—they're also heavily optimized for these types of state change operations, since they're so fundamental to the applications using them. Different frameworks take different approaches to handling the changing states of components. For example, some take a more automated approach, requiring more overhead in monitoring for changes in state. Others are more explicit in that the state is explicitly changed, and as a direct result, events are fired. The latter approach requires more discipline on the part of the programmer, but also requires less overhead.

There are two things we can do to avoid performance issues that might occur as we scale up the number of our components and their complexity. First, we can make sure that we're only maintaining state for things that matter. For example, if we set up handlers for changes in state that never happen, it's wasteful. Likewise, if we have components that change state and fire events that never result in a UI update, it's also wasteful. Though difficult to spot, if these hidden gems can be avoided, we'll also avoid future scaling issues related to responsiveness.

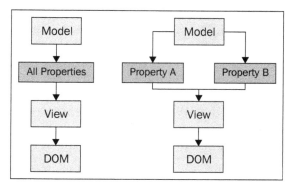

Views can react the same to any model property change; or, they can have specialized responses to specific property changes. Virtual DOMs attempt to automate this process for us.

Dealing with side-effects

In the preceding section, we looked at the states that components maintain, and how they can hurt performance if we're not careful. So how do these changes in state come about? They don't happen spontaneously—something explicitly has to change the value of a variable. This is called a side effect, something else that has the potential to hurt performance, and is unavoidable. Side effects are what cause the changes in state we covered in the previous section, and they too can hurt performance if not treated with care.

The opposite of a function with side effects is a pure function. These take input and return output. Nothing changes state in between. Functions such as these have what's known as **referential transparency**—which means that for a given input, we're guaranteed the same output, no matter how many times we call the function. This property is important for things like optimization and concurrency. For example, if we're always going to get the same result for a given input, the temporal location of the function call really doesn't matter.

Think about generic components that our application shares with components that are specific to features. These are less likely to maintain state—the state is more likely to be in components that are closer to the DOM. Functions in these top-level components are good candidates for implementations free of side effects. Even our feature components could potentially implement side-effect-free functions. As a rule of thumb, we should push our state and side effects as close to the DOM as possible.

As we saw in *Chapter 4, Component Communication and Responsibilities*, it's difficult to mentally trace what's happening in a convoluted publish/subscribe event system. With events, we don't really need to trace these paths, but with functions, it's a different story. The challenge is that if our function changes the state of something, and that causes a problem elsewhere in the system, it's very difficult to track that sort of issue down. Additionally, the more side-effect-free functions we use, the less sanity checking code that's needed. We often come across bits of code that check the state of something, seemingly for no reason. The reason—that's what made it work. This approach can only get one so far with scaling up the development effort.

Following is an example that shows a function with side effects, versus a function *without* side effects:

```
// This function mutates the object that's
// passed in as an argument.
function withSideEffects(model) {
    if (model.state === 'running') {
        model.state = 'off';
    }

    return model;
}


// This function, on the other hand, does not
// introduce side-effects because instead of
// mutating the "model", it returns a new
// instance.
function withoutSideEffects(model) {
    return Object.assign({}, model, model.state === 'off' ?
        { state: 'running' } : {});
}

var first = { state: 'running' },
    second = { state: 'off' },
    result;

// We can see that "withSideEffects()" causes
// some unexpected side-effects because it
// changes the state of something that's used
// elsewhere.
result = withSideEffects(first);
console.log('with side effects...');
```

```
console.log('original', first.state);
console.log('result', result.state);

// By creating a new object, "withoutSideEffects()",
// doesn't change the state of anything. It can't
// possibly introduce side-effects somewhere else in
// our code.
result = withoutSideEffects(second);
console.log('without side effects...');
console.log('original', second.state);
console.log('result', result.state);
```

DOM rendering techniques

Updating the DOM is expensive. The best way to optimize DOM updates is to not update them. In other words, as infrequently as possible. The challenge with scaling up our application is that DOM manipulations become more frequent, out of necessity. There's more state to monitor, and more things that we need to notify the user about. Even so, in addition to the techniques employed by our frameworks of choice, there're things we can do with our code to lighten the load on DOM updates.

So, why exactly are DOM updates so expensive, relative to plain JavaScript that's running in the page? The computations that take place to figure out what the display should look like, eat a lot of CPU cycles. We can take steps to ease the load on the browser render engine, and improve the responsiveness of our UI, using techniques in our view components that require less work from the rendering engine.

For example, reflows are rendering events that result in a whole class of computations that need to be made. Essentially, reflows happen when something about our element changes, which could result in changes to the layout of other nearby elements. The whole process cascades throughout the DOM, so a seemingly inexpensive DOM operation could result in quite a lot of overhead. Rendering engines in modern browsers are fast. We can get away with a little sloppiness in our DOM code, and the UI will perform perfectly. But as new moving parts are added, the scalability of our DOM rendering techniques comes into play.

So the first strategy to consider is, which view updates can result in reflows? For example, changing the content of elements is not a big deal and will likely never cause performance problems. Inserting new elements into the page, or altering the style of existing elements in response to user interactions — these have potential for responsiveness issues.

One DOM rendering technique that's trendy today is using a **virtual DOM**. ReactJS and similar libraries leverage this concept. The idea is that our code can just render content into the DOM, as though it's rendering the whole component for the first time. The virtual DOM intercepts these rendering calls and figures out the difference between what's already rendered, and what's changed. The name virtual DOM comes from the fact that a representation of the DOM is stored in JavaScript memory, and this is used to make comparisons. This way, the real DOM is only touched when absolutely necessary. This abstraction allows for some interesting optimizations, while keeping the view code minimalistic.

Sending one update after another to DOM isn't ideal either. Because the DOM will receive the list of changes to make and apply them sequentially. For complex DOM updates that have the potential to trigger reflow after reflow, it's better to detach the DOM element, make the updates, and then reattach it. When the element is reattached, the expensive reflow calculations are done at once, rather than several times in succession.

However, sometimes the DOM itself isn't the problem — it's the single-threaded nature of JavaScript. While our component JavaScript is running, there's no chance for the DOM to render any pending updates. If our UI is unresponsive in certain scenarios, it's best to set a timeout to let the DOM update. This also gives any pending DOM events a chance to be processed, which is important if the user is trying to do something while there's JavaScript code running.

Next is an example that shows how to defer running JavaScript code during CPU-intensive computations, giving the DOM a chance to update:

```
// This calls the passed-in "func" after setting a
// timeout. This "defers" the call till the next
// available opportunity.
function defer(func, ...args) {
    setTimeout(function() {
        func(...args[0]);
    }, 1);
}

// Perform some expensive work...
function work() {
    var i = 100000;
```

```
    while (--i) {
        for (let c = 0; c < 100; c++) {
            i * c;
        }
    }
}

function iterate(coll=[], pos=0) {
    // Eat some CPU cycles...
    work();

    // Update the progress in the DOM...
    document.getElementById('progress').textContent =
        Math.round(pos / coll.length * 100) + '%';

    // Defer the next call to "iterate()", giving the
    // DOM a chance to display the updated percentage.
    if (++pos < coll.length) {
        defer(iterate, [ coll, pos ]);
    }
}

iterate(new Array(1000).fill(true));
```

Web Workers are another possibility for long-running JavaScript code. Because they can't touch the DOM, they don't interfere with the responsiveness of it. However, this technology is beyond the scope of this book.

API data

The last major obstacle that will hit us with performance issues as we continue to scale, is the application data itself. This is an area we have to be especially mindful of, because there are so many scaling influencers at play. More features doesn't necessarily translate to more data, but it often does. That's more types of data, and more data volume. The latter is mostly influenced by the growing user base of our software. Our job as JavaScript architects is to figure out how we can scale our application to deal with both the increased load time, and the increased size of our data once it arrives at the browser.

Load latency

Perhaps the biggest risk to scaling our application's performance is the data itself. The way our application data changes and evolves over time is somewhat of a phenomenon. The features we add in the frontend certainly influence the shape of our data, but our JavaScript code doesn't control the number of users or the way they interact with our software. These latter two points can lead to an explosion in data, and if our frontend isn't prepared, it will grind to a halt.

The challenge we face as frontend engineers is that there's nothing to display for the user when we're waiting for data. All we can do is take the necessary steps for providing an acceptable *loading* user experience. Which begs the question—while we're waiting for data to load, do we block the whole screen with a loading message, or do we show loading messages piecemeal for the elements that are waiting on data? With the first approach, there's little risk of the user doing something that's not allowed, because we prevent them from interacting with the UI. With the second approach, we have to worry about the user interacting with the UI while there are outstanding network requests.

Neither approach is ideal, because at any point while data is loading, the responsiveness of our application is fundamentally constrained. We don't want to completely block the user from interacting with the UI. So, maybe we need to enforce a strict timeout for data loading. On the plus side, we're guaranteeing responsiveness, even if the response is to inform the user that the backend is taking too long. The down side is that sometimes waiting is necessary, as far as the user is concerned, if something needs to get done. Sometimes, the bad user experience is preferable—instead of unintentionally creating an even worse experience.

There are two things that the frontend needs to do to help scale our backend data. First, we need to cache responses where possible. This reduces the load on the backend, and also improves the responsiveness for the client with the cached data, since it doesn't have to make another request. Obviously, we need some kind of invalidation mechanism in place, because we don't want to cache stale data. Web sockets are a good candidate solution here—even if they only notify the frontend sessions that a particular entity type has changed, so that the cache can be cleared. The second technique to help with growing datasets is to reduce the amount of data that's loaded with any given request. For example, most API calls have options that let us constrain the number of results. This needs to be kept to a reasonable number. It helps to think about what the user needs to look at first, and design around that.

Working with large data sets

In the preceding section, we went over some of the scaling issues we face in frontend development concerning application data. As our application grows, so does the data, presenting a loading challenge. Once we've managed to get the data into the browser, we still have lots of data to work with, which can lead to unresponsive user interactions. For example, if we have a 1000 item collection, and an event passes this structure around to several components for processing, the user experience is affected. What we need are tools that help us transform data that's big and difficult to scale across several components, into something that's filtered down to just the essentials.

This is where low-level utility libraries come in handy — complex transformations on large data sets. Larger frameworks might expose similar tools — they're likely using low-level utilities under the hood. The transformations we'll want to perform on our data are of the map-reduce variety. That's the abstract pattern anyway, functional programming libraries such as Underscore/lodash, provide many variations on this pattern. How does this help us scale with large data sets? We can write clean reusable mapping and reducing functionality, while deferring much of the optimizations to these libraries.

Ideally, our application would only load the data it needs for rendering the current page. A lot of the time this simply isn't possible — the API can't account for every possible query scenario required by our features. So we use the API to filter broadly, then when the data arrives, our components filter the data using more specific criteria.

The scaling problem here is the confusion between what's being filtered by the backend, and what's filtered in the browser. If one component relies more on the API, while other components do most of their filtering locally, it leads to confusion amongst developers, and non-intuitive code. It can even lead to unpredictable bugs if the API changes, even subtly, since our components are using it differently.

The less time that's spent mapping or reducing, the more responsive the UI feels to the user. This is why it's important that we get only the data that the user sees, as early on as possible. For example, we don't want to pass around API data in an event as soon as it arrives. We need to structure our component communication in such a way that the computationally expensive filtering on large collections happens as soon as possible. This lightens the load for all the components, since they're now working with a smaller collection. So scaling to more components isn't a big deal because they'll have less data to process.

Optimizing components at runtime

Our code should be optimized for the common case. This is a good scaling tactic because as more features and users are added to the mix, it's the common cases that grow, not the edge cases. However, there's always the possibility that we'll have two equally common cases to deal with. Think about deploying our software to a number of customer environments. Over time, as features evolve to meet customer requests, there could be two or three common cases for any given piece of functionality.

If we have two functions that deal with the common case, then we have to figure out which function to use at runtime. These common cases are extremely course-grained. For example, a common case might be "collection is large" or "collection is small". Checking for these conditions isn't expensive. So if we're adaptable to the common case as it changes, our software will be more responsive than if we weren't adaptable to changing conditions. For example, if the collection is large, the function could take a different approach to filtering it.

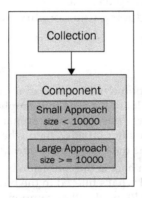

A component can alter it's behavior at runtime, based on broad
classifications such as small or large collections

Summary

Responsiveness, from the user's perspective, is a strong indicator of quality. Unresponsive user interfaces are frustrating to work with, and are unlikely to require any further scaling efforts on our part. The initial load of the application is the first impression the user has of our application, and it's also the most difficult to make fast. We looked at the challenges of loading all our resources into the browser. This is a combination of modules, dependencies, and build tools.

The next major hurdle to responsiveness in JavaScript applications are the inter-component communication bottlenecks. These usually result from too much indirection, and the design of the events required to fulfill a given feature. The components themselves can also serve as bottlenecks to responsiveness, because JavaScript is single-threaded. We went over several potential issues in this space, including the cost of maintaining state, and the cost of dealing with side effects.

The API data is what the user cares about, and the user experience degrades until we have it. We looked at some of the scaling issues posed by an expanding API and the data within. Once we have the data, our components need to be able to quickly map and reduce it, all while the data set continues to grow as we scale. Now that we have a better idea of how to make our architecture perform well, it's time to look into making it testable and functional in a variety of contexts.

8

Portability and Testing

Web applications have come a long way from only a few years ago. Gone are the days when JavaScript code was embedded, sort of as an afterthought, inside a webpage. In today's web, we build JavaScript applications, and if you're reading this book, applications that scale. This means our architecture needs to be designed with portability in mind; the idea that the backend that serves our application and feeds it data, is replaceable.

Along with portability comes the idea of testability. We can't make assumptions about the backend when we're developing large scale JavaScript code, and that means having the ability to run with no backend at all. This chapter looks at these two closely related topics and what they mean for us in the face of changing scaling influences.

Decoupling the backend

If we need any further motivation that JavaScript is no longer just for scriptable web pages, look no further than NodeJS. It doesn't require the full browser environment, just the V8 JavaScript engine. Node was created primarily as a backend server environment, but it still serves as a great showcase for how far JavaScript as a language has come. In the same vein, we want our code to be portable, running with any backend infrastructure we can throw at it.

In this section, we'll look at the reasons why we want to loosen the coupling between our frontend JavaScript code, and the APIs it talks to in the backend. We'll then introduce the first steps to mocking APIs, negating the need for a backend entirely.

Mocking the backend API

If we're developing a large scale JavaScript application, we'll have the beginnings of a backend infrastructure. So why then, would we consider detaching our code from that backend so that it no longer depends on it? It's always a good idea to support loosely coupled components when striving for something that scales, and that's true of the coupling between the frontend and backend environments in a web application. Even if the backend API never changes, we can never assume that the technologies and the frameworks used to build the API never will. There are other benefits to loosening this dependency too—like the ability to update the UI independently of the rest of the system. But the main scaling benefit to mocking our backend APIs comes from the development and testing perspectives. There's simply no substitute for being able throw together new API endpoints and hammer them with requests. Mock APIs are the crash test dummies for our JavaScript code.

Like it or not, it sometimes feels like we're creating demo-ware—in the middle of a development sprint, we have to show off what we have to an interested stakeholder. Rather than letting this lead to despair, we'll gain confidence from our mock data. Demoing is no longer a big deal, and with the confidence of our mocked data, we'll start to view these events as little challenges for ourselves. Of course, we always have to maintain the outward appearance of a heroic programmer—for management's sake!

Given how awesome mock data is, what are the downsides? Like anything else in our product, it's a piece of software that has to be maintained—and that always carries risk. For example, the mock API loses some of its value if it falls out of sync with the actual API, or if it creates confusion between what's functional in the UI versus what's mocked. To deal with these risks, we have to put processes in place around how we design and implement our features, which we'll go over here shortly.

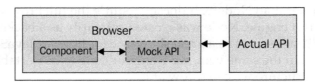

The mock API sites outside of any component that communicates with the actual API; when the mock is removed, the component doesn't know any better

Frontend entry points

Where does the seam of our frontend meet with the backend? This is where we'd like to make the switch, between mock data and what's normally returned by the API. The seam might actually be located behind the web server — in which case we're still making real HTTP requests, just not interacting with the real application. In the other case, we're mocking entirely within the web browser, where HTTP requests are intercepted by the mocking library handlers before they ever leave the browser.

In both kinds of mocking, there's a conceptual seam between our frontend application — which is what we're trying to establish. This is key, once we find it, because it represents our independence from the backend. It's not that there's anything wrong with being tightly coupled to the backend in production — that's what it's there for. In other circumstances, such as during development, being able to orchestrate what happens when our components send API requests is a crucial scaling tactic.

There's the possibility of creating mock data modules using models and collections directly. For example, if we're running in mock mode, we would import this module and we'd have mock data to work with. The problem with this approach is that our application knows it's not really working with the backend. We don't want that. Because we want our code to run as though it's running in a production environment. Otherwise we're going to experience some side effects of manually instantiating the mocks — it needs to be as far-removed from our actual code as possible.

Whichever mocking mechanism we decide to go with, it needs to be modular. In other words, we need the ability to turn it off and take it out of the build entirely. In production environments, there should be no mocks. In fact, our mocking code shouldn't even be present in production builds. This is a little easier to achieve if our mocks are served up by a web server. If our mock handlers reside in the browser, we need to take them out somehow, which requires a build option of some sort. There'll be more on build tools later on in the chapter.

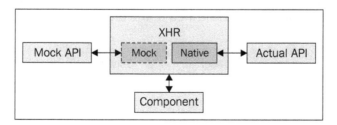

Mocking API requests in the browser, intercept calls at the XHR level. If there's mocking code there, it will look for mock APIs. When the mock is taken out, the native HTTP requests function as usual.

Mocking tools

As mentioned in the preceding section, there're two main approaches to mocking the backend API. The first approach involves bringing in a library such as Mockjax into our application to intercept XHR requests. The second approach is having a real HTTP server in place, but one that isn't actually touching the real application—it serves up mock data the same way as the Mockjax approach.

The way Mockjax works is simple yet clever. It works under the assumption that the application is using jQuery `ajax()` calls to make HTTP requests, which is a fairly safe assumption since most frameworks use this under the hood. When Mockjax is called, it overrides some core jQuery XHR functionality with its own. This is run whenever an XHR request is made. It checks if there's a route spec that matches the requested URI, and will run the handler if one is found. Otherwise, it'll just pass through and attempt making a request to the backend—which is kind of useful if we wanted to combine real API requests with mocked requests. We'll dig into that combination later.

Any given handler can return JSON data, or any other format for that matter, just as our real API would. The key is that our core code—our models and collections that initiate the requests—know nothing about Mockjax because it's all happening at a lower layer. The same model and collection code runs unmodified against the production backend. All we have to do is *unplug* the module where Mockjax is called when deploying against the real API.

We can achieve the same property—running unmodified code—using the mock web server technique as well. It's actually the exact same idea as hijacking the XHR requests, only done at another level. The main advantage being that we don't have any special steps to take during deployment. It's either a mock server or a real one, and in production environments, it's unlikely there's a mock server running. The disadvantage is that we do need a server running, which isn't a lot to ask—it is an added step though. And we do lose a little bit of portability. For example, we can package up a mock build and send it to someone. If it doesn't require a web server, the entire application can be demonstrated in the browser.

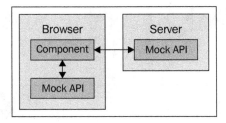

Mocking APIs from the browser, or behind a web server; both approaches achieve the same result–our code doesn't know it's talking to a mock.

Generating mock data sets

Now that we know what the options are for declaring the mocked API endpoints, we need data. Assuming our API is returning JSON data, we could store our mock data in JSON files. For example, the mock module can pull in these JSON modules as dependencies, and the mock handlers can use them as a data source. But where does this data come from?

As we start building mocks, there's most likely an API in existence, running somewhere. Using our browser, we can look at the data returned by various API endpoints and manually curate our mocked data. This process is a lot simpler if the API is documented, because then we'll have a clue as to the allowable values for any given field in any given entity. Sometimes we don't actually have a starting point for the creation of our mock data—we'll go over that in the feature design process section.

The advantage of manually creating our mock data sets like this is that we can ensure that it is accurate. That is, we don't want to create something that's not reflective of the data we're mocking, because that would defeat the whole purpose. Not to mention the scaling bottleneck of keeping up with changes in the API. What would be nice, is using a tool to automate the task of generating mock data sets. It would just need to know the schema for a given entity and it could take care of the rest, accepting a few arguments and throwing in some randomness for good measure.

Another useful mock data generation tool would be something that extracts the real API data from a given deployment, and stores them as JSON files. For instance, say there's a staging environment where our code is showing signs of issues. We could run our data extraction tool against that environment to get the mock data we need. Since we want to leave the staging environment more or less intact, this approach is safe since any damage we do to the mock data while diagnosing, is in memory and easily wiped clean.

Performing actions

One challenging aspect of implementing mock APIs is performing actions. These are requests other than GET, and usually need to change the state of some resource. For example, changing the value of a resource property, or removing a resource entirely. We need some common code that our handlers can leverage to perform these actions, since our API endpoints should follow the same patterns when it comes to performing actions on them.

How manageable this is to actually implement depends on the complexity of our API action workflow. An easy to implement action would be modifying the property value of a resource then returning 200 successful. However, our application most likely has more complex workflows, such as long-running actions. For example, these types of actions might return the ID of a newly created *action* resource, and from there, we'll need to monitor the state of that action. Our frontend code already does this, since that's what it needs to do with the real API—it's the mock where we need to implement these subtleties of our application.

The actions can get quite messy, fast. Especially if the application is a large one, with lots of entity types, and lots of actions. The idea is to strive for the minimum viable success path for mocking these actions. Don't go into great detail in trying to simulate, step by step, everything the application does—it doesn't scale.

Feature design process

We're not creating mock APIs for the fun of it, we're creating them to aid in the development of features. Given that we could have a rather large API, and thus lots to mock, we need a process in place that somewhat governs the order in which we do things. For example, do we need to wait for an API to be in place before we go ahead and start implementing a feature? If we can mock the API, then we shouldn't have to, but the API itself still needs to be designed, and there are lots of API stakeholders.

In this section we'll go over some of the necessary steps to ensure that we're using mocks correctly, and in a way that scales alongside our feature development.

Designing the API

Some API endpoints are generic enough to support multiple features. These are the entities that are central to our application. Typically, there're a handful of entities that play a vital role, and most features use them. On the other hand, most new features we develop will require an expansion of our API. This could mean one new API endpoint, or several. It's a question of how our backend resources are composed, and this involves some level of design work.

The problem with trying to scale our feature development is that implementing a new API could take a really long time. So if we need the API in place before we start working on the frontend feature, we end up delaying the feature, which isn't ideal. We want to start working on something while it's fresh. If something sits in a backlog as a to-do, it often stays there forever. Having a mock API in place for the proposed feature lets us get the ball rolling without delay, which is crucial for scaling development.

When we implement the mock of a new API endpoint, we enter greenfield design territory. This means that we have to take into account the considerations of those who may not necessarily do frontend development. And we may or may not touch the actual implementation of the real API—it all depends on our team structure. That said, whoever the subject matter experts are, they'll need transparent access into the design of our proposed API. They can provide suggestions, changes, and so on. There's no point in continuing down the path of the impossible. Another approach might be to get a backend programmer to sketch out a possible API spec. This is strictly big picture stuff; only the essential endpoints with minimal properties and actions. The rest are details that can easily be changed in our mocks and in our actual code after the fact.

Implementing features using mock APIs before the backend code is touched, can help prevent costly mistakes. For example, let's say we implement some feature in the frontend, using mock APIs, to the point where it's demonstrable. This gives other engineers with specific backend domain knowledge an opportunity to call out the infeasibility of the feature, and we get to avoid avoid making a costly mistake in the future.

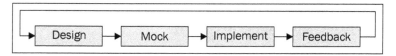

The cycle of designing a mock API, and implementing features against it

Implementing the mock

Now that we've been tasked with implementing a feature, the first step is implementing a mock API to support the development of our frontend code. As we saw in the preceding section, we should be interacting closely with whoever will ultimately implement the real API. The first step is to figure out what the API will look like at a high level. The rest we can fine-tune as we move closer to having to implement the real API.

However, we don't always have to depend on the API team members for hand-holding during the development of our mocks. We probably have some API endpoints, and they're probably already used by some of our frontend components. That said, there's probably a discernible pattern that we can follow, especially if the mock is just another mundane entity type that we just happen to be missing. If we follow a good pattern, then that's a good starting point because there's less chance of radical changes later on.

When we know what our mock API looks like, and what we can do with it, we need to populate it with mock data. If we have tools in place that generate data for other mocks, we need to figure out how to extend that. Or, we need to just manually create some test entities to get started. We don't want to spend a lot of time up-front entering data. We only need the minimum viable number of entities to prove our approach is feasible.

> We might not always want to start off with the actual mock endpoint before creating the data. Instead, we may want to work from the data upward—designing the right entity rather than worrying about the mechanics of the API itself. This is because, the data ultimately needs to be stored somewhere, which is an important activity. Working on the data lets us work in a different mindset. Choose the approach that best fits the task at hand.

The mocks we create aren't always creating something brand new. That is, the API we're mocking may already exist, or the implementation of it is underway. This actually makes the mock much easier to implement, because we can ask the API author for sample data, or help in general, in order to build our mocks. Remember, if we want to be portable, we have to be able to remove the frontend from the backend, which means we'll need to mock the API in its entirety.

Implementing the feature

Now that we have our mock API in place, it's time to profit. It's not all said and done—the mock APIs are tweaked all the time. But it's enough for us to get going with the real frontend code. And right away, we'll find problems. These could be problems with the proposed API, or problems with the component that talks to the API. We can't let these discourage us, because that's exactly what we're looking for— early problem detection. You just don't get this without mock APIs.

If the API is generally acceptable, and our component code works, we could discover performance bottlenecks in our design. This is especially easy to find if we have tools that generate mock data for us, because it's nothing to generate 100,000 entities, and see what happens with our frontend code. Sometimes this is a quick refactoring, other times it's a complete change in approach. The point is that we need to find these issues earlier rather than later.

Something else we can do with mocks that's otherwise difficult is to demo often. That's not easy to do when we're heavily dependent on a large backend environment with lots of overhead. If it takes less than a couple minutes to get a feature up and running for demonstration, we can confidently show off what we're doing. Maybe it's wrong, maybe the stakeholders think of something they missed, having seen their idea come to life. This is how mocks help us scale the feature development life cycle through early and continuous feedback.

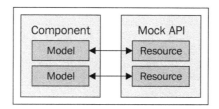

The internals of a component under development, communicating with mock API endpoints

Reconciling mock data with API data

At this point, the feature is implemented, and how we reconcile the mock we've created for our feature depends on the state of the real API. For example, if we're just mocking something in the API that's been around for a while, then it's safe to assume nothing needs to happen as long as there's high fidelity between our mock and the real thing. However, if we're mocking a greenfield API, there's a good chance that something will have changed, even subtly. It's important that we capture these changes to make sure our existing mocks stay relevant in subsequent releases.

This is the part of the mocking process that's tough to scale, and generally unpleasant. There're so many different ways that our mocks can get out of sync with what's in the real API, it's daunting to even try to keep up. If we have tools for generating mocks, it's a lot easier. We might even be able to generate the entire API based on specs the API team creates. But this is problematic too, because while the mock generation can be automated, the specs themselves need to be created, somewhere, somehow. So it might be best to implement a tool that can generate mock data, but have our own code process requests. As long as we don't repeat ourselves too much, and the API has a decent pattern, we should be able to keep up with our mocks.

Another possibility is turning off certain mock API endpoints while leaving others on. Think of it as a sort of pass through—where the granularity of mock endpoints can be specified, instead of only being able to toggle the entire mock API. For example, this capability could come in handy if we're trying to troubleshoot a specific problem in our application, and we'll need to coax certain API endpoints to return specific responses in order to replicate the problem. We can do this in libraries such as Mockjax, because requests that don't match a request path spec are just forwarded on to the native XHR mechanism.

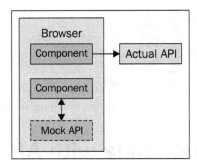

One component uses a mock API, while another uses the actual API

Unit testing tools

It's time to turn our attention to testing, having covered the basics of mocking API endpoints at scale. Our ability to mock APIs is highly relevant to testing our code, because we can test against those same mocks, or at least the same data. This means that if our tests fail, we can start interacting with the UI if we need to, using the same data that failed the test, trying to figure out what's happening.

We'll look into using the unit testing tools that ship with JavaScript frameworks, and figure out where their value lies. We'll also look at using more generic standalone testing frameworks that run with any code. We'll close out the section with a look at how our tests can be automated, and how this automation fits into our development workflow.

Tools built into frameworks

If we're using one of the larger, all-encompassing JavaScript application frameworks, there's a good chance that it will ship with some unit testing tools. These aren't meant to replace the existing unit testing tools that are framework-agnostic. Rather, they're meant to augment them — providing specific support for writing tests in the flavor of the framework.

What that ultimately means for us is writing less unit test code. If we're following the patterns of the framework, then there're lots of unit testing tools that already know about our code. For example, if it already knows the types of components we'll be using to implement our features, then it can stub out tests for us. This is a huge help, not having to repeat ourselves, and it leads to us ultimately getting more test coverage on our code.

In addition to generating the skeleton of our tests for us, framework testing facilities can provide utility functions for us to use within our tests. This means less unit test code for us to maintain, and this is only possible because the framework knows what kinds of things we'll want to do within our tests, and can abstract them out for us in the form of utility functions.

The challenge with relying on framework-specific testing tools is that we'll be coupling our product with a specific framework. This is unlikely to be a problem for us, because once a framework is chosen, we're going to stick with it, right? Well, not necessarily. Not in today's tumultuous JavaScript ecosystem. Part of being portable requires a level of agility in our architecture, meaning we have to be adaptable to change. This is perhaps why more of today's projects rely less on mega frameworks and more on a composition of libraries.

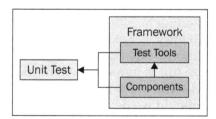

Unit test is tightly coupled to components and unit testing tools from the framework

There's a lot of asynchronous code in large-scale JavaScript applications, and this async code shouldn't be ignored by our unit tests. For example, we need to make sure that our model units are able to fetch data and perform actions. These types of functions return promises, and we want to ensure that they resolve or fail as expected.

This is much easier to achieve with a mock API in place. Using either the in-browser approach or the web server approach is fine, because our code still treats them as real asynchronous operations. Something else we might consider mocking is a web socket connection. This is a little trickier to do in the browser because we have to override the built-in web socket class. We can use a real web socket connection to test with if our mock sits behind a web server.

Either way, mocking web sockets is difficult, because we have to mock the logic that triggers web socket messages in response to something else happening, such as an API action. However, we still might want to consider mocking web sockets after we have more basic test coverage, because if our application depends on them, it's important to automate tests for them.

Standalone unit testing tools

Another approach to unit testing tools is to use a stand-alone framework. That is, a unit testing tool that doesn't care which JavaScript application framework or libraries we're using. Jasmine is the standard for this purpose, as it provides a clean and concise way for us to declare test specifications. Out-of-the-box, it has a test runner that works in the browser, which gives us nicely formatted output for tests that pass, and tests that fail.

Most other stand-alone unit testing facilities use Jasmine as their base, and extend it to provide additional capabilities. For example, there's the Jest project, which is essentially Jasmine with additional capabilities such as module loading and mocks built-in. Again, something like this is framework-agnostic; it's focused purely on the tests. Using these types of stand-alone tools for unit testing is a good portability tactic, because it means that should we decide to move to different technologies in our code, our tests will still be valid and can actually help make the transition run smoothly.

Jasmine isn't the only game in town, it's simply the most generic and gives us a lot of freedom in how we structure our tests. Qunit, for instance, has been around for a long time. It's applicable to any framework, but was originally conceived as a testing tool for jQuery projects. We might even want to roll our own testing tools, should we feel that the available testing tools are too heavy, and don't give us the kind of flexibility or the kind of output our project needs. Something we probably don't want to write ourselves is a test runner. Our unit tests aren't run haphazardly, whenever we feel like it. They're often part of a large chain of tasks we want to automate.

Some code is more testable than other code. This simply means that depending on how our components are structured, it may be easy to break them down into testable units, or it could be difficult. For example, code with a lot of moving parts, and a lot of side effects means that we have to write a relatively large suite of tests for this component if we want decent test coverage on it. If our code is loosely coupled, with relatively few side effects, it will be much easier to write tests for.

While we want to strive for testable code, to make the process of writing unit tests easier, it isn't always possible. So if it means sacrificing coverage, sometimes that's the better option. We want to avoid re-writing code, or worse, changing around the architecture we're happy with, for the sake of writing more tests. We should only do this if we feel that our component is sufficiently large that it deserves more test coverage. If it gets to this point, we should probably re-think our design anyway. Good code is naturally easy to test.

Toolchains and automation

As our application grows more large and complex, a lot needs to happen "offline", as part of the ongoing development process. Running unit tests is just one task we want to automate. For example, before we even run our tests, we'll probably want to use a tool that lints our code to ensure we're not committing anything too sloppy. After the tests pass, we might need to build our component artifacts, so they can be used by a running instance of our application. If we're generating mock data, this might also be part of the same process.

Collectively, we have a toolchain that can automate all of these tasks for us. These tasks are often smaller steps in a larger, more coarse-grained task, like *build production* or *build develop*. Larger tasks are just a composition of smaller tasks, as defined by us. This is a flexible approach because the **toolchain** can handle the sequence of tasks, in the order they need to happen, or, we can just run tasks piecemeal. For instance, we might only want to run tests.

The most popular toolchain is a task runner called Grunt. Other similar tools, such as Gulp, are gaining traction too. What's nice about these tools is that they have a thriving ecosystem of plugins that do much of what we need—we just need to configure the individual tasks that use these plugins, and the larger tasks that we want to compose. It takes very little effort on our part to setup a toolchain that can automate much of our development process—pretty much everything aside from writing the code itself. Without toolchains, it ranges from very difficult to impossible, to scale our development efforts to more than just a few contributors.

Another bonus of using toolchains for automated tasks is that we can change the type of artifacts we're building on-the-fly. For example, when we're right in the middle of developing a feature, we won't necessarily want to build the production artifacts with every change. Doing so can really slow us down, in fact. It's better if our tools can just deploy the raw source modules, which can also make debugging a lot easier too. Then when we're closer to being done, we start with the production builds, and test against those. Our unit tests can run against both the raw source code and the resulting artifact builds—because we never know what can be introduced after compilation.

Testing mock scenarios

The more our application scales, the more scenarios it'll have to deal with. This is the result of more users using more features, and all the ensuing complexity our code has to handle. Having mock data and unit tests can really help put these scenarios to the test. In this section, we'll go over some of the options available to us for creating these mock scenarios and then testing them, both with our unit tests and by interacting with the system as a user.

Mock APIs and test fixtures

Mock data is valuable to us for many reasons, one of which is unit tests. If we're mocking the API, we can run our unit tests as though our code is hitting a real API. We have fine-grained control over individual data points in our mock data, and we're free to change it how we see fit—it's sandboxed data, it has no negative effect on the outside world. Even if we're generating our mock data using a tool, we can get in there and shuffle things about.

Some unit testing tools accept fixtures, data used for the sole purpose of running the tests. This isn't all that different from the data we would use with an API mocking tool like Mockjax. The main difference is that fixtures aren't much use to us outside of the unit testing framework that consumes them.

Well, what if we could use it for both testing and mocking? For instance, say that we want to utilize the fixture data capabilities of our unit testing framework. It's got some automated features that we couldn't use if we didn't feed it fixture data. On the other hand, we also want to mock the API for development purposes, interacting with the feature, detachment from the backend, and so on. There's nothing stopping us from feeding the fixture data into both the unit tests, and into the API mocks. That way, we could use any mock data generators we've created to generate scenarios that are shared by our tests, and by the user interactions in the browser.

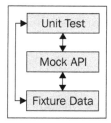

Unit tests can hit the mock API with requests, or use fixture data directly; if the mock API serves
the same data, then it's easier to figure out what's wrong with failed tests

Scenario generation tools

Over time we'll accumulate new features and more scenarios in which our customers will use those features. Therefore, it would be immensely helpful to have, as part of our toolchain, a utility for generating mock data. Taking things a step further, this utility could accept arguments for generating mocks. These could be simply course-grained arguments, but that's usually all we need to turn randomly generated mock data into a curated scenario we need.

The individual mock scenarios we'll generate won't vary a great deal from one another. That's kind of the point—we need something that serves as a baseline, so that if we do make interesting discoveries about our scenarios, we can ask—*what's different about this data?* If we do start generating lots of scenarios because we have a tool that enables us to do so, we need to make sure we do in fact have a "gold" mock data set—which is something that we know works as expected.

The types of changes we would need to make to the gold mock data are things like changing the number of entities in a collection. For example, let's say we wanted to see how something performs on a given page. So we create a million mock entities, and see what happens. The page breaks entirely — further investigation reveals a `reduce()` function that tries to sum a number greater than the maximum safe integer. Scenarios can reveal interesting bugs like this. Even if the scenario we're using is far fetched and unlikely to occur in production, we should still fix the bug because other less extreme scenarios could certainly trigger it.

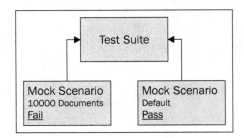

Changing the scenario can cause our tests to fail; usually we create scaling scenarios to see where our code falls apart

There's a huge number of possibilities we could simulate. For example, we could mangle some of the data by deleting properties from entities, ensuring that our frontend components have sane defaults for things it expects, or that it fails gracefully. This latter point is actually really important. As we scale our JavaScript code, there're more and more scenarios that we cannot fix, and we just have to make sure our failure mode is acceptable.

End-to-end tests and continuous integration

The final piece of the puzzle is putting together end-to-end tests for our feature, and hooking it into our continuous integration process. Unit tests are one thing, they leave us confident that our components are solid — when they pass. Users don't care about unit tests, end-to-end tests serve as a proxy for our users that interact with our UI. For instance, there's probably a set of use cases embedded within the requirements of any given feature we implement. The end-to-end tests should be designed around these.

Tools like Selenium make automating end-to-end tests possible. They record the test as a set of steps we perform as a user. Those same steps can then be repeated whenever we tell it to. For example, an end-to-end test might involve the creation, modification, and deletion of a resource. The tool knows what to look for in the UI as a success path. When this doesn't happen, we know the test has failed, and there's something we need to go fix. Automating these types of tests is essential to scaling, as the number of ways users can interact with our application grows as we add features.

We can look to our toolchain for help here once more, since it's already automating all our other tasks, it should probably automate our end-to-end tests as well. The toolchain is essential for our continuous integration process as well. We'll probably share a CI server that builds other aspects of our system as well, only they're done differently. The toolchain makes it easy for us to integrate with a CI process, because we simply need to script the appropriate toolchain commands.

Having mock data in place can help us run end-to-end tests, because if the tool is going to behave as a user would, it's going to have to make backend API requests. This gets us consistency, and helps us rule out the tests themselves as being problem sources. With mock APIs, we can develop unit tests, and end-to-end test against the same source.

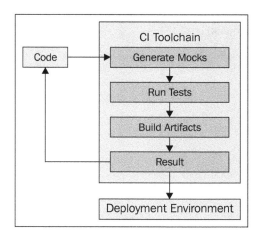

The toolchain, the mock data, and our tests, all running in a CI environment; the code we're developing is the input

Summary

This chapter introduced the concept of portability in frontend JavaScript applications. Portability in this context means not being tightly coupled with the backend. The main advantage of being portable means that we can treat our UI as its own application, it doesn't require any specific backend technologies to be in place.

To help our frontend achieve independence, we can mock the backend API it depends on. Mocking also lets us focus strictly on UI development—eliminating the possibility of backend issues from hindering our development.

Mocks can help us test our code as well. There're a number of unit testing libraries, each with their own approach, that we can utilize. If we're using the same mock data to run our tests, then we can rule out inconsistencies with what we see in the browser. Our tests need to be automated, alongside several other tasks that take place as part of our development process.

The toolchain we implement fits in nicely with a continuous integration server—an essential scaling tool. This is also where end-to-end tests are automated, which gives us a better idea of what the user will encounter when they use our software. Now it's time to switch gears and take a hard look at the limits of scaling our application. We can't scale up infinitely, and the next chapter will look at how to avoid hitting a wall, as we scale beyond a certain size.

9
Scaling Down

We tend to think of scaling as a unidirectional problem—we can only scale up from where we are currently. Unfortunately, that doesn't quite work. We can only scale in one direction for so long before the foundation crumbles under our feet. The key is in identifying the scaling limitations, and designing around them.

In this chapter, we'll look at the fundamental scaling constraints faced by JavaScript architects in nearly every browser environment. We'll also look at the customer as a scaling influencer, and how new features conflict with existing features. Scaling down from bloated design is an essential activity as well.

The composition of our application as a whole determines how easy or how difficult it'll be to scale down by turning features off. It all has to do with coupling, and if we look closely, we'll often discover that we need to refactor our components so they can be easily removed later on.

Scaling constraints

Our applications are constrained by the environments in which they run. This means the hardware on which the client is running, and the browser itself. What's interesting about web applications is that there's also the transmission of the code itself to consider. For example, if we're writing backend code, we can throw more code at any problem we face, and that's not a problem because that code doesn't move around—it runs in one place.

With JavaScript, size matters. There's simply no way around this fact. As a corollary, network bandwidth matters — both for the delivery of our JavaScript artifacts, and our application data from the API.

In this section, we'll address the hard scaling constraints imposed on us in the browser computing environment. As our application grows, we feel the pressure of these constraints more and more. Each of these needs to be considered when planning new features for our application.

JavaScript artifact size

The cumulative size of our JavaScript artifacts can only grow so much. Eventually, the load time of our application will suffer to the point that nobody will want to use our application. Huge JavaScript artifacts are typically indicative of bloat in other areas. For example, if we're delivering huge files to the browser, we probably have too much of something. Maybe we don't need the features nobody uses, or maybe there's repetitious code spread throughout our components.

Whatever the cause, the effects aren't good. Smaller is always better. How do we know when the file size of our JavaScript artifacts are small enough? That depends — there's no universal *ideal* size. Where is our application deployed, on the public internet? Behind a VPN for corporate users? There may be different acceptance criteria for the users of these types of systems. Broadly speaking, the public internet users are going to be less forgiving of poor load time performance and feature bloat. The corporate users on the other hand, generally appreciate more features and are more tolerant of lackluster load times.

The biggest contributor to growing JavaScript artifact sizes are the new features we constantly add to our product. These result in new components which add weight. Any given feature is going to have a minimum set of files, each for the components that follow the pattern of our existing features. If our patterns are half decent, then we should be able to keep the size of our components reasonable. However, repetitive code always finds its way into the application when deadlines are involved. Even if our code is as lean as it could possibly be, we still have to implement features when they're asked for.

Compiled artifacts help us with the size problem. We can concatenate and uglify files, saving on the number of network requests, and the overall bandwidth. But, any given feature will keep these compiled artifacts growing. We can keep growing for some time before encountering any problems. As stated, the problems are relative, depending on the environment, and the users of our software. In all cases, the size of our JavaScript artifacts cannot grow infinitely.

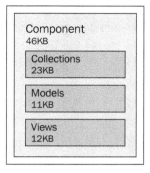

The size of JavaScript artifacts are the aggregate result of all modules that make up the component

Network bandwidth

The size of our JavaScript artifacts contributes to the overall network bandwidth consumption of our application. Especially as there's more user uptake—users are the multipliers for all our architectural woes. Coupled with our JavaScript code, is our application data. These API calls also contribute to the overall network bandwidth consumption, and user-perceived latency.

> As our application scales geographical boundaries, we'll notice a diverse range of connectivity issues. In many parts of the world, high-speed networks simply aren't an option. If reaching these markets is important to us, and it should be, then our architecture needs to cope with slow internet connections. Using CDNs to deliver the libraries our application use can help here because they take into consideration the geographical location of the requests.

The challenge is that any new feature is going to add new network bandwidth consumption. There's the size of the code, and the new API calls introduced by the new component. Mind you, these effects aren't felt immediately. For example, the new component doesn't make API calls on page load, only when the user navigates to a specific URI.

Nonetheless, new API endpoints mean more aggregate network bandwidth usage over time. Further, it's not just a matter of making one API call when a user navigates to a feature page. It sometimes takes a tangle of three or more API calls, in order to construct the data to be presented. We need to keep this in mind when we're thinking that a new API call isn't a big deal, as it usually ends up being more than one call, and that means more bandwidth consumption.

Is there a fundamental network bandwidth limit? Not theoretically, but it's like the size of our JavaScript artifacts—we can grow them to 10MB each if we please. All we can say with confidence is that it's not going to improve the user experience, and the side effects could cause a much worse experience. The same goes with network bandwidth consumption.

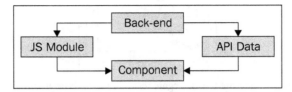

Components consume network bandwidth by requesting JavaScript modules and API data

'Following is an example that shows how the aggregate latency of our application suffers as more requests are made:

```
// model.js
// A model with a fake "fetch()" method that doesn't
// actually set any data.
export default class Model {

    fetch() {

        // Returns a promise so the caller can work
        // with this asynchronous method. It resolves
        // after 1 second, meant to simulate a real
        // network request.
        var promise = new Promise((resolve, reject) => {
            setTimeout(() => resolve(), 1000);
        });

        return promise;
    }

};

// main.js
import Model from 'model.js';

function onRequestsInput(e) {
    var size = +e.target.value,
        cnt = 0,
```

```
        models = [];

    // Create some models, based on the "requests"
    // number.
    while (cnt++ < size) {
        models.push(new Model());
    }

    // Setup a timer, so we can see how long it
    // takes to fetch all these models.
    console.clear();
    console.time(`fetched ${models.length} models`);

    // Use "Promise.all()" to synchronize the fetches
    // of each model. When they're all done, we can stop
    // the timer.
    Promise.all(models.map(item => item.fetch())).then(() => {
        console.timeEnd(`fetched ${models.length} models`);
    });
}

// Setup our DOM listener, so we know how many
// models to create and fetch based on the "requests"
// input.
var requests = document.getElementById('requests');

requests.addEventListener('input', onRequestsInput);
requests.dispatchEvent(new Event('input'));
```

Memory consumption

With every feature we implement, the memory consumed by the browser grows. This may seem like an obvious statement, but it's important. Memory issues not only hurt application performance, they can crash the entire browser tab. Therefore, we need to pay close attention to the memory allocation characteristics of our code. The profiler built into the browser can record the allocations of objects in memory over time. This is a useful tool for diagnosing issues, or for general observations about how our code behaves.

Frequently creating and destroying objects can cause performance lags. This is because the objects that are no longer referenced, are garbage collected. When the garbage collector is running, none of our JavaScript code runs. So we have a conflicting requirement—we want our code to run fast, and we don't want to waste memory.

The idea is to not cause the garbage collector to run unnecessarily. For example, there are times where we can hoist the variable up to a higher scope. This means that the reference isn't created and destroyed several times throughout the lifetime of the application.

Another scenario is with frequent allocations in a short timeframe, such as within a loop. While JavaScript engines are smart about dealing with these types of scenarios, they're still worth keeping an eye out for. The best resources are the source code of low-level libraries that take into account the garbage collector, and avoid unnecessary allocations.

The responses returned from the API also consume memory, and depending on the data returned, a substantial amount of memory. Something we'll want to do is ensure that there's a cap on how much data a given API endpoint can respond with. Many backend APIs do this automatically, not returning more than a 1000 entities at a time. If we need to make our way through the collection, then we need to provide an offset argument. However, we may want to further constrain the size of the API response, because the size of individual entities in the collection could occupy a lot of memory as a model in the browser.

While these collections are typically garbage collected as the user moves around from page to page, each new feature we implement presents the opportunity for subtle memory leak bugs. It's the subtle bugs that are difficult to deal with because the leaks are slow and manifest themselves differently across environments. When the memory leak is large and obvious, it's easier to reproduce, and thus, easier to locate and fix.

Next is an example that shows how quickly memory consumption can get out of hand:

```
// model.js
var counter = 0;

// A model that consumes more and more memory,
// with each successive instance.
export default class Model {

    constructor() {
        this.data = new Array(++counter).fill(true);
```

```
    }

};

// app.js
// A simple application component that
// pushes items onto an array.
export default class App {

    constructor() {
        this.listening = [];
    }

    listen(object) {
        this.listening.push(object);
    }

};

// main.js
import Model from 'model.js';

function onRequestsInput(e) {
    var size = +e.target.value,
        cnt = 0,
        models = [];

    // Create some models, based on the "requests"
    // number.
    while (cnt++ < size) {
        models.push(new Model());
    }

    // Setup a timer, so we can see how long it
    // takes to fetch all these models.
    console.clear();
    console.time(`fetched ${models.length} models`);

    // Use "Promise.all()" to synchronize the fetches
    // of each model. When they're all done, we can stop
    // the timer.
    Promise.all(models.map(item => item.fetch())).then(() => {
        console.timeEnd(`fetched ${models.length} models`);
    });
```

```
}

// Setup our DOM listener, so we know how many
// models to create and fetch based on the "requests"
// input.
var requests = document.getElementById('requests');

requests.addEventListener('input', onRequestsInput);
requests.dispatchEvent(new Event('input'));
```

CPU consumption

One of the big factors in how responsive our user interface feels, is the CPU on the client. If it's available to run our code whenever there's code to be run, in response to a click for instance, then the UI will feel responsive. If the CPU is busy handling other things, our code will have to sit there and wait. And so will the user. Obviously there's a lot of software asking for the CPU's attention in a given operating environment—much of which is completely out of our control. We can't scale down the use of other applications outside of the browser, but we can scale down the use of the CPU from within our JavaScript application. But first, we have to understand where these JavaScript CPU cycles come from.

At the architectural level, we don't think about micro optimizations that make little sections of a single component more efficient. We care about scaling down, which translates to a noticeable effect on the CPU consumption while our application is running. We saw, in *Chapter 7, Load Time and Responsiveness*, how to profile our code. This tells us where the CPU is spending it's time in our code. With profiles as our measuring stick, we can proceed to make changes.

The two factors that influence the use of the CPU at an architecturally significant level are the number of active features, and the amount of data that's used by these features. For example, as we add more components to our system, there's naturally more CPU consumption, because when things happen in the UI, the component code for that feature needs to respond in some way. But this isn't likely to have a big impact on its own. It's the API data that comes with implementing a new feature that makes that CPU cost dangerously expensive.

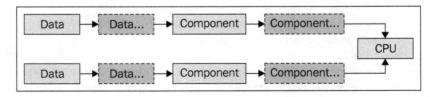

Combining forces that eat CPU cycles—more data, processed by more components

For example, if we were to keep implementing new features and the data set never changed, we would start to feel the CPU cost. This is because there's more indirection, meaning more code to run for any given event that takes place. This slow down would happen at glacial speeds however — we could just keep adding hundreds and hundreds of features, without breaking a sweat, CPU-wise. It's the changing data that makes this a scaling impossibility. Because if you multiply the number of features by the growing data sets, the CPU cost grows exponentially.

Well, maybe not *all* our features are consuming *all* of our data. And maybe there's very little indirection in our design. It's still the biggest factor to consider when it comes to scaling down. So if we need to cut CPU costs, we need to remove features and the data they process — it's the only way to get a measurable impact.

Following is an example that shows how the number of components, combined with the number of data items, progressively consumes more CPU time:

```js
// component.js
// A generic component used in an application...
export default class Component {

    // The constructor accepts a collection, and performs
    // a "reduce()" on it, for no other reason than to eat
    // some CPU cycles.
    constructor(collection) {
        collection.reduce((x, y) => x + y, 0);
    }

}
// main.js
import Component from 'component.js';

function onInput() {
    // Creates a new collection, the size
    // is based on the "data" input.
    var collection = new Array(+data.value).fill(1000),
        size = +components.value,
        cnt = 0;

    console.clear();

    // Sets up a timer so we can see how long it
    // takes for x components to process y collection items.
    console.time(`${size} components, ${collection.length} items`);

    // Create the number of components in the "components"
```

```
        // input.
        while (cnt++ < size) {
            new Component(collection);
        }

        // We're done processing the components, so stop the timer.
        console.timeEnd(`${size} components, ${collection.length} items`);
    }

// Setup out DOM event listeners...
var components = document.getElementById('components'),
    data = document.getElementById('data');

components.addEventListener('input', onInput);
data.addEventListener('input', onInput);

components.dispatchEvent(new Event('input'));
```

Backend capabilities

The final scaling constraint we'll address is the backend that serves our static resources and our API data. This is a limiting factor because our code can't run until it reaches the browser, and we can't display information for the user until the raw data has arrived. These two things are up to the backend to deliver on, but there are a few things to keep in mind about the backend when doing frontend development.

The first concern is the usage of our application. Just as the browser running our JavaScript code can't scale infinitely up, neither can our backend APIs. While they have some characteristics that enable them to scale up that browsers don't, they still feel the impact of more request volume. The second concern is the way that our code interacts with the API. We have to look at the how a single user uses our application, and look at the API requests generated from those interactions. If we can optimize the requests made for one user, adding more users will have less of an impact on the backend.

For example, we don't want to make requests that we don't need to. This means, *don't load data until it's actually needed.* And, *don't load the same data over and then over again.* If a user doesn't start interacting with a feature till five minutes into their session, that frees up the backend to service other requests during that interval. Sometimes our components use the same API endpoints. What if they're both created at the same time, and both send the same API request in succession? The backend has to service both requests, unnecessarily, because they're going to have the same content.

We need to structure component communication to account for scaling influencers such as the load generated in the backend. In this particular instance, the second component could look up in a *pending requests* map and return that promise instead of generating a completely new request.

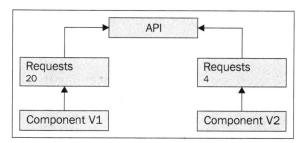

Newer components should aim to consume less bandwidth; one approach is to accomplish the same functionality using fewer API requests

Conflicting features

The lines between our features become blurred as our software grows. There's bound to be at least some overlap, and that can be a good thing. If there wasn't at least a little overlap, users would have a tough time transitioning from one area of our UI to another. This becomes a problem when we reach a feature threshold where there're multiple overlapping layers that just keep overlapping. It's a self-propagating problem that get's worse with every new feature added, till it is addressed.

Two potential causes of this problem include parts of our application that grow irrelevant over time, and instead of being retired, they sit around and get in the way. Customer demand plays a big part in this scaling influence because it determines the future direction of the product. This should also give us an indication of what's in place now, that either needs to change in order to meet demand, or needs to go away in the near future.

Overlapping functionality

Over the course of our application's life, there's going to be new functionality that overlaps with existing functionality. That's just the nature of software development— building on what you already have, not starting something way out left-field that has nothing to do with our existing features. What's nice is when that overlap is unobtrusive, and serves as a bridge from existing features to new features and enhancements.

Where this overlap doesn't work so well is when it conflicts with existing features. It's like trying to build a house in the woods, without removing any trees first. One of two things needs to happen if the overlap is going to be seamless and scalable. Either we need to adjust what's already in place in order to accommodate what's coming down the line, or we need to rethink the new functionality so that it better fits in the available space. It's interesting, because given what we have, we sometimes have to scale down features before they're even implemented — this is often easier than after they've been implemented.

The end result of nonsensical feature overlap is something that the user finds clunky and difficult to use, so we can expect some complaints down the road. It is something else that we'll likely have to fix or remove later on. We actually tell ourselves this quite often — it's not a great addition, but it's good enough for the deadline. But at what cost is it *good enough*? In addition to the forecasted user frustration, there's also the code to worry about. Rarely do we say things like — *well, the users may not like it, but the code is fantastic*. The poor user experience is often the result of poor feature planning, followed by poor implementation.

The solution is quite simple, as we've already seen. It's a matter of making room for the changes, or altering the new feature. Something we often neglect is documenting the potential problems. For example, if we see a problem with a planned feature fitting in with our current code, we need to speak up and generate an outline of what doesn't fit where and why. It's always better to have this information archived and searchable than to ignore it. This is how we scale our architectural ideas, by being inclusive with the team.

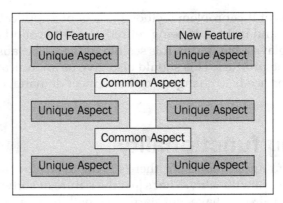

Overlap between old features and new features is a good starting point for scaling down unnecessary code

Irrelevant features

Over time some features prove their worth. Our users love them, and use them often. What's more—we hardly have to maintain them. They just work. On the other hand, some of the other features we've implemented start to rust sooner than we would have liked. There could be any number of signs that this is taking place. Maybe a handful of users love the feature, but it's buggy and difficult to maintain. Maybe the majority of our users love the feature but it's preventing a number of initiatives from taking place in the project. But the most common case is that nobody is really using it.

Whatever the reason, features do become irrelevant. Our problem, as an industry, is that we like to hoard code. Sometimes we keep around irrelevant functionality out of necessity—we would simply break too many things, or introduce backward incompatibility where we need it. Other times, and this really is a frontend problem more than anywhere else, we keep the feature around because we don't have an explicit mandate to rid ourselves of it. Well that needs to happen if we want to scale our application I'm afraid.

It's a matter of being proactive rather than reactive. As we know, every component contributes to our scaling constraints—be it network, memory, CPU, or otherwise. Who knows, maybe we could get by just fine with the feature sitting around in our product. It's better to get it out of the way, because there's less chance of it actually constraining our ability to scale. We may think it's a harmless piece of code, but isn't it better to rule it out completely? Further, it's simply a good attitude to instill in everyone around us—scale down the things we don't need, then think about where to go from there. If we set the precedent with all our stakeholders that we're ready and willing to trim the fat, we're more likely to convince them to ship a leaner product.

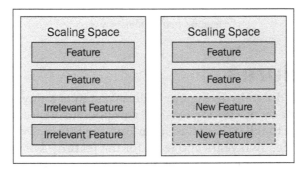

There's only so much room for our application to scale; removing irrelevant features frees up scaling space

Customer demand

Depending on the type of product we're building, and the type of users it's servicing, customer demand will translate to either disciplined planning and implementation, or to knee-jerk reactions. We all want to make our customers happy — that's why we're building the software. But it's these quick decisions to implement stuff people are screaming for that detracts from our architecture. It's like we're implementing the features as though they were bugs. With bugs, we implement quick fixes as quickly as possible because we need to get them out the door.

New features aren't bugs. Despite what users and management say — they'll live another day without the functionality they're asking for. We need to find a way to buy ourselves the time necessary to fit the new features customers want into our architecture. That's not to say that we can keep putting it off — we have to do so in a timely manor. Perhaps excising existing features that users care less about is the fastest way forward.

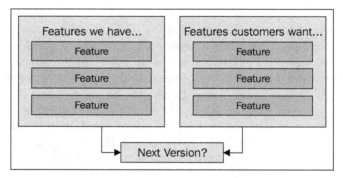

Figuring out which features make it into the next version; they're either features we already have, or new features that customers want

Design failures

It's one thing to scale down by fixing our code as it stands today. For example, by taking features out, or by modifying existing components to accommodate newly planned features. But that'll only get us so far into the future. Design ideas that seemed like a good idea two years ago were for the features we were thinking about two years ago, some of which may no longer be around today.

To make a lasting impact on our architecture, we have to repair broken patterns. They still work in our product because we make them work, even though they may not be the best tools for the job. Figuring out the right design isn't a one time event, it happens as our software changes, and as our scaling influences command.

In this section we'll look at a few ways we might address some flaws in our design. Perhaps there're a lot of moving parts we don't need. Perhaps we're processing our API data inefficiently, due to the complexity of our component communication model. Or maybe the structure of our DOM elements is leading to obtuse selector strings and slowing down development. These are just a handful of possibilities — defective patterns vary project by project.

Unnecessary components

When we'll first set out to design our architecture and build our software, we'll leverage patterns that make sense at the time. We design our components to be loosely coupled with one another. To get this loose coupling, we often make a trade-off — more moving parts. For example, to keep the responsibilities of each component focused, we have to split larger components into smaller ones. These patterns determine the composition of our feature components. If we're following this pattern, and it has unnecessary parts, anything new we develop will also contain unnecessary parts.

It's difficult to get patterns right, because when we need to decide on which patterns to use, we don't have enough information. Frameworks, for example, have very generic patterns in place because they serve a much broader audience than our application does. So while we want to utilize the same patterns exposed by the framework, we need to adapt them to our specific features. These are the patterns that change, gradually, as customer demand shifts the nature of our product. We can embrace this natural phenomenon, and invest the time in fixing our patterns. Or, we can go about fixing the issues as they arise, keeping our original patterns intact. Being amenable to changing what we once assumed was foundational is the best way to scale our architecture.

The most common pattern flaw is unnecessary indirection. That is, components that are abstract, and don't really have any value. While they decouple a component from something else, that's about all they do. We'll notice that over time, our code accumulates these modules that are relatively small, and tend to all look the same. They're small because they don't do much, and they look the same because they're part of the pattern we promised to be consistent with throughout our code. At the time that the pattern was conceived, this component made perfect sense. After having implemented several components, it makes less sense. Losing the component doesn't detract from the design, and in fact, the whole project feels a little lighter now. It's funny, the disconnect between what patterns look like on paper, and what they look like in a real application.

Next is an example that shows a component that uses a controller, and another version of the component that doesn't require a controller and has one less moving part:

```javascript
// view.js
// An ultra-simplistic view that updates
// the text of an element that's already in
// the DOM.
export default class View {

    constructor(element, text) {
        element.textContent = text;
    }

};

// controller.js
import events from 'events.js';
import View from 'view.js';

// A controller component that accepts and configures
// a router instance.
export default class Controller {

    constructor(router) {
        // Adds the route, and creates a new "View" instance
        // when the route is activated, to update content.
        router.add('controller', 'controller');
        events.listen('route:controller', () => {
            new View(document.getElementById('content'),
'Controller');
        });
    }

};

// component-controller.js
import Controller from 'controller.js';

// An application that doesn't actually do
// anything accept create a controller. Is the
// controller really needed here?
```

```
export default class ComponentController {

    constructor(router) {
        this.controller = new Controller(router);
    }

};

// component-nocontroller.js
import events from 'events.js';
import View from 'view.js';

// An application component that doesn't
// require a component. It performs the work
// a controller would have done.
export default class ComponentNoController {

    constructor(router) {
        // Configures the router, and creates a new
        // view instance to update the DOM content.
        router.add('nocontroller', 'nocontroller');
        events.listen('route:nocontroller', () => {
            new View(document.getElementById('content'), 'No
Controller');
        });
    }

};

// main.js
import Router from 'router.js';
import ComponentController from 'component-controller.js';
import ComponentNoController from 'component-nocontroller.js';

// The global router instance is shared by components...
var router = new Router();

// Create our two component type instances,
// and start the router.
new ComponentController(router);
new ComponentNoController(router);

router.start();
```

Inefficient data processing

Micro-optimizations don't really buy us much in efficiency. Duplicate processing on the other hand can lead to massive scaling problems. The challenge is that we might not even notice that there's duplicate processing going on until we look for it. It often happens when data is passed from one component to another. The first component performs transformations on the API data. Then, the raw data is passed to the second component, which then proceeds to perform the exact same transformations. As more components are added, these inefficiencies start to add up.

The reason we seldom catch these types of problems is that we're blinded by our beautiful design patterns. Sometimes the inefficiencies that hurt the user experience are masked by our code because we're doing things consistently. That is, we're keeping the relationships between our components loosely coupled, and because of this, our architecture scales in a number of respects.

The majority of the time, a little bit of repetitive data processing is a perfectly acceptable trade-off. It depends on what it gains us in terms of flexibility for dealing with other scaling influences. For example, if we're able to easily handle a number of different configurations, and enable/disable features where we need to, because of the number of disparate deployments we have, then this trade off might make sense. However, scaling in one regard often means *not* scaling in another. For example, the amount of data is likely to increase, meaning the data that's passed around from component to component will increase. So the duplicitous data transformations that weren't a problem, are now a big problem. When this happens, we have to scale down our data processing.

Again, this doesn't mean we need to start introducing micro-optimizations—it means we have to start hunting for the big efficiency wins. The starting point should always be with the network calls themselves, because not getting the data in the first place is the biggest efficiency win for the frontend. The second place to look at is the data that's getting passed around from component to component. This is where we need to make sure that a component isn't doing the exact same thing as the previous component in the chain.

Following is an example that shows a component that will fetch model data each time `fetch()` is called. It also shows an alternative implementation that doesn't fetch the model when there's already a pending request:

```
// model.js
// A dummy model with a dummy "fetch()" method.
export default class Model {

    fetch() {
        return new Promise((resolve) => {
```

```
        setTimeout(() => {

            // We want to log from within the model
            // so that we know a fetch has actually
            // been performed.
            console.log('processing model');

            // Sets some dummy data and resolves the
            // promise with the model instance.
            this.first = 'First';
            this.last = 'Last';

            resolve(this);
        }, 1000);
    });
}

};


// component-duplicates.js
import Model from 'model.js';

// Your standard application component
// with a model.
export default class ComponentDuplicates {

    constructor() {
        this.model = new Model();
    }

    // A naive proxy to "model.fetch()". It's
    // naive because it shouldn't fetch the model
    // while there's outstanding fetch requests.
    fetch() {
        return this.model.fetch();
    }

};

// component-noduplicates.js
import Model from 'model.js';

// Your standard application component with a
```

```
// model instance.
export default class ComponentNoDuplicates {

    constructor() {
        this.promise = null;
        this.model = new Model();
    }

    // "Smartly" proxies to "model.fetch()". It avoids
    // duplicate API fetches by storing promises until
    // they resolve.
    fetch() {

        // There's a promise, so there's nothing to do -
        // we can exit early by returning the promise.
        if (this.promise) {
            return this.promise;
        }

        // Stores the promise by calling "model.fetch()".
        this.promise = this.model.fetch();

        // Remove the promise once it's resolved.
        this.promise.then(() => {
            this.promise = null;
        });

        return this.promise;
    }

};

// main.js
import ComponentDuplicates from 'component-duplicates.js';
import ComponentNoDuplicates from 'component-noduplicates.js';

// Create instances of the two component types.
var duplicates = new ComponentDuplicates(),
    noDuplicates = new ComponentNoDuplicates();

// Perform two "fetch()" calls. You can see that
// the fetches are both carried out by the model,
// even though there's no need to.
duplicates.fetch();
duplicates.fetch().then((model) => {
    console.log('duplicates', model);
```

```
});

// Here we do the exact same double "fetch() call,
// only this component knows not to carry out
// the second call.
noDuplicates.fetch();
noDuplicates.fetch().then((model) => {
    console.log('no duplicates', model);
});
```

Making duplicate API calls is tough to avoid when our components are decoupled from one another. For example, let's say that one feature creates a new model, and fetches it. Another feature that's on the same page needs the same model, but knows nothing about the first component—it too creates it and fetches data.

These result in the exact same API call being made, which is obviously unnecessary. Not only is it inefficient for the frontend because it has two separate callbacks for the exact same data, it's also hurting the system as a whole. When we make requests that aren't needed, we're clogging up the request queue in the backend, affecting other users. We have to keep an eye out for these types of duplicate calls and adjust our architecture accordingly.

Excessively creative markup

The markup used to render our UI components can grow a little out of control. Because we're aiming for a specific look and feel, we have to hack the markup a little in order to do that. Then we hack it some more, because it doesn't look quite right on this browser or that browser. The result is elements deeply nested in other elements, to the point where they've lost any semantic meaning. We should strive for semantic use of tags—a test goes in p elements, a clickable button is a button element, the page sections are split by section elements and so on.

The challenge here is that the design we're going for is usually expressed as a wireframe, and we need to implement it in such a way that it can be sliced up into pieces that our framework and components can use. So the simplicity gets lost as trying to keep things semantic, and at the same time dividing into standalone views isn't always feasible.

We have to try to simplify the DOM structure where we can though, because it has a direct impact on the simplicity and the performance of our JavaScript code. For example, our components often need to find elements on the page, either to change their state or to read values from them. We can write selector strings that query the DOM and return the elements we need. The strings are found all throughout our view code, and they reflect the complexity of our markup.

When we stumble across convoluted selector strings in our code, even the ones we wrote ourselves, we have no idea what it's actually querying for—because the DOM structure and the tags used are of no help. So it turns out that using semantic markup can actually be of great help to our JavaScript code. There're also the performance implications of complex DOM structures—if we're frequently traversing deep DOM structures, we're pay a performance penalty.

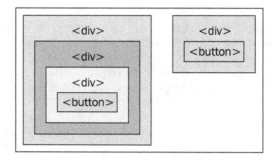

Excessively deep element nesting can usually be scaled down, to not use so many elements

Application composition

We'll close out the chapter with a section on application composition. This is the 10,000 foot view of our application, where we can see how individual features fit. In *Chapter 3, Component Composition* we looked at component composition, and the same principles apply here. The idea being that we're operating at a slightly higher level.

In *Chapter 6, User Preferences and Defaults* we looked at configurability, and this is also relevant to the idea of application composition. For example, turning features off, or turning on features that are disabled by default. The composition of our application as a whole has a huge impact on our ability to scale down certain aspects.

Feature enablement

The expedient approach to scaling down is turning features off. The difficult part is getting stakeholders to agree that this is a good idea. Then we can just remove the feature, and we're all set, right? Not necessarily. We may have to spend some time taking the feature out. For example, what if it touches several entry points into the system and there's no configuration that can switch these off? It's no big deal, it just means we need more time spent on writing code that takes these out.

The only problem is with testing the effects of taking the feature out of the system. For the scenario where there's no configuration that'll do the job, we have to spend time writing code that will do it, before we even get to test it. For instance, we could spend five minutes turning off configuration values, and then we'll get immediate results. Maybe we learn early on that there's a lot of work that needs to be done before we can safely remove the feature from the system.

In addition to testing the runtime behavior of our application once a feature has been removed, we'll probably want some build-time options as well. If our production code is compiled into a handful of JavaScript artifacts, then we need a way to completely remove these features from the build. It's one thing to disable components through configuration. That means when our code runs, certain things won't load, and so on. If we take the feature out of our source code repository, then 'it's obviously less of a concern—our tools can't build what isn't there. However, if we have hundreds of potential components that can be included in our build artifacts, we need a way to exclude them.

New feature impact

The next major impact on our application is the addition of new features. Yes, this discussion is about scaling down, but we can't ignore the addition of new features into our application. This is, after all, why we're scaling down in the first place. Not to build a smaller application that does less. It's to make room for features our customers want, and to improve the overall quality of our product over time.

The processes of adding features and removing features often happen in parallel. For example, during a development sprint, while one team implements a new feature, another team is responsible for the removal of a feature that's causing problems. Since both of these activities affect the application in major ways, we have to be considerate, and minimize these effects.

Essentially, that means making sure that the removal of the old feature isn't too disruptive to the new feature that's being added. For example, what if the new feature depended on something from the old feature. If our design is sound, then there won't be any direct dependencies. However, complexity is not well understood by humans—especially cause and effect through indirection. So scaling this operation might mean that we don't perform the two activities in parallel after all.

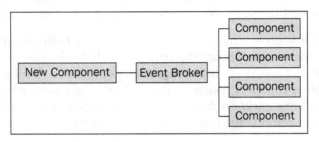

Depending on our inter-component communication model, the effects of adding new components into the system should be fairly subdued

Essential libraries

The last pieces that impact the composition of our application are the frameworks and libraries we're using. It goes without saying that we only want to use what we need—use it or lose it, so to speak. This is mainly an issue when we're pulling in smaller libraries as dependencies. Frameworks, by contrast, are all inclusive for the most part. This means that everything you need is likely in the framework already. While this isn't necessarily true, it still helps us reduce the number of dependencies on third-party libraries.

Even frameworks are modular nowadays, meaning we can cherry-pick the goodness we want and leave the rest alone. Even still, it's easy to bring in components, from a framework or otherwise, that we won't really use. This happens quite a lot in web site development. We need this one piece of functionality, and we don't want to write it ourselves because that library over there already does it. Then it gets lost in the mix of pages. We should learn the lesson that web sites didn't—our applications need a focused set of dependencies, essential to getting the job done.

Summary

This chapter introduced the notion that not everything in our application is infinitely scalable. In fact, nothing about our application is infinitely scalable, as each aspect is constrained by different factors. These factors all blend together in unique ways, and it's up to us to make the necessary trade-offs. If we want to keep scaling up, we have to scale down in other areas.

New features come from customer demand, and they often overlap with other features we've already implemented. This could be because we haven't defined the new feature very well, or because the existing entry points into the system aren't very well defined. Either way, this can make for a challenging exercise; the removal of existing features, in place of a new feature. We often need to remove the areas of overlap, as they cause confusion both at the code level and the usability level.

Scaling down isn't just a piece by piece activity — there are the design patterns to think about as well. After we've removed a feature, we need to look at the patterns we're using and ask, *do we want to keep having to do this in the future?* The better, more scalable path forward, is to fix the pattern. Even after we've scaled down, there's always the potential for error. In the following chapter, we'll take a closer look at failing components, and how to deal with them.

10
Coping with Failure

At this point in the book, we would like to think that our architecture is sound. We've thought about scale, and made all the appropriate trade-offs, sacrificing performance for configurability, and so on. The one aspect of scalable JavaScript architectures we have yet to go into any depth on is the human factor. As smart as we are, we're the weakest link because we design the application and write the code—and we're really good at making subtle mistakes.

Until we're taken out of the software development equation completely, we have to design our components with failure in mind. This involves thinking about the failure modes—do we fail fast, or do we try to recover from the error? It involves thinking about the quality of our errors—some errors are easier to work with than others. But it's also about understanding our limitations; we can't feasibly detect and recover from every conceivable error.

As we scale our application, the approaches of how we deal with failures need to scale too. This is yet another trade-off we need to make amongst the many other scaling influences. Let's start by looking at the fail-fast failure mode.

Failing fast

Systems or components that fail-fast, stop running when they fail. This may not sound like a desirable design trait, but consider the alternative: a system or a component that fails, but then continues to run anyway. These components could be running in an erroneous state, whereas, that's not possible if the system or component halts.

There are times where we'll want to recover a failed component, and we'll get into that topic later on in the chapter. In this section, we'll go over some of the criteria used in determining whether a JavaScript component should fail fast, and what the consequences are for the user. Sometimes, even our fail-fast mechanisms fail us, which we also need to consider.

Using quality constraints

When our components fail-fast, it's usually due to a known error state. On the other hand, something completely unexpected could happen. In either case, it's likely to leave our component in a bad state, and we don't want the application to carry on like everything is fine. Let's focus on failing-fast when quality constraints aren't met. These are assertions about how our application behaves. For example, we shouldn't try sending API requests more than three times; we wouldn't wait more than 30 seconds for a response—this property of a model should always have a non-empty string, and so on.

When these assertions prove false, it's time to stop executing—either the one component, or the whole system. It's not as though we're doing this to annoy the user. Like any failure, we hope they happen as infrequently as possible. Think of failing-fast as the airbags deploying in a car accident—when that happens, our car is no longer drivable.

The decision to make a component or the system as a whole fail fast under certain conditions shouldn't be taken lightly. For example, if we fail fast in one place because a feature team implemented it thusly, for reasons unknown to other teams, the whole application starts to fail. Meanwhile, it turns out that this is by design, and is expected behavior. There needs to be strict rationale for this failure mode. What really helps with discussion around fail-fast scenarios are the catastrophic results that could potentially happen if the application were to continue on undeterred.

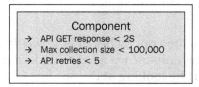

Constraints that when violated, cause the component to fail-fast, possibly causing
the whole application to fail fast

Providing meaningful feedback

We don't want to give users, or other members of our development team the wrong idea about why our software isn't running under certain scenarios. This means that we have to distinguish between failing-fast, and total uncontrolled failure. The latter is something that breaks our application, and may cause the browser tab to crash. Or worse, it's still alive, crawling around on the floor, giving the user the impression that it still kind of works, doing harm all the while.

This means that when we fail fast, we have to make it glaringly obvious to the user that something has stopped working, and they shouldn't continue using it. Whether it's a single component that failed or the entire application, we have to make the messaging clear and concise. The user doesn't always need to know what went wrong; they just need to know that the component or the application is currently broken, and anything they do, will not work.

This is actually an important consequence of introducing fail-fast into our architecture—we get responsiveness under certain conditions. We never leave the user guessing. Sure, it's annoying to have broken software in front of us, but not as annoying as waiting, trying, and waiting some more, to find out it's broken. With a clear message stating that the application isn't working, or parts of it aren't, we may want to physically prevent the user front interacting with it. For example, by throwing a `div` overlay on top of the elements or by turning off the DOM event handlers.

Next is an example that shows two error handlers. The first implicitly handles the error by disabling the button. The other callback does the same thing, but also explicitly displays an error message:

```
// The DOM elements...
var error = document.getElementById('error'),
    fail1 = document.getElementById('fail1'),
    fail2 = document.getElementById('fail2');

// The first event merely disables the button.
function onFail1(e) {
    e.target.disabled = true;
}

// The second event disables the button, but
// also explicitly informs the user about what
// went wrong.
function onFail2(e) {
    e.target.disabled = true;
    error.style.display = 'block';
}

// Setup event handlers...
fail1.addEventListener('click', onFail1);
fail2.addEventListener('click', onFail2);
```

When we can't fail fast...

We can design fail-fast mechanisms into our components. What we can't do is guarantee that these mechanisms themselves won't fail. That is, the code we write to protect us from ourselves is written by us. And so on, and so on. We could keep writing layer after layer of error handling code that fails fast and gracefully when there's a failure in the layer beneath it. But to what end?

Understanding that we can't always fail predictably is part of the scaling challenge we face. Because, at some point, we have to focus on the features we're actually trying to provide, and not the scaffolding that keeps it up. Extraneous failure handling code doesn't make our product any better, it just adds bulk in the form of code. If we try to stay focused on the features we're building, the obvious cases where we want to fail fast will reveal themselves.

The problem with failure detection code is that it needs to scale with the rest of our application, with the external scaling influencers guiding its evolution. For example, more users mean more demand on the backend. This means there's a very real possibility that our failure detection code will never arrive—how do we account for this scenario? We don't. Because trying to solve problems like these, doesn't scale. Trying to prevent them from happening in the first place is a more fruitful endeavor.

Fault tolerance

Systems that are fault-tolerant have the ability to survive a malfunctioning component. This is done by either correcting the error in the component, or by replacing the defective one with a new instance. Think of fault tolerance as an airplane with the ability to land using only one engine—the passengers are our users.

Typically, we hear about fault tolerance in the context of large scale server environments. It's a viable concept in frontend development too, given sufficient complexity. In this section, we'll start off by thinking about how to classify components into critical versus noncritical components. Then we'll move on to detecting errors, and how to go about handling the error so that the application can continue to function.

Classifying critical behavior

Just like there're critical sections of code that can't be interrupted, by another thread for example, there're components that can't fail gracefully in our application. Some components just have to work, no matter what, and if they don't, then they need to fail-fast to avoid causing further damage. This is why we need to classify our components as such. While it may seem obvious that a given component has to be functioning as expected, it makes sense to consistently classify them somehow. It's a good idea to socialize ideas like this throughout the organization.

When we know which components are critical, we know that they just have to work, and there's no conceivable situation from which they'll need to recover. If these components fail, there's a bug that needs to be fixed. We can also target these critical components more heavily with unit tests.

It's not a good idea to have tiers of criticality for components. For example, a level for components that are absolutely critical, and the next level of components that are not critical but too important to be deemed regular, and so on—it defeats the purpose. We can either survive without the component, or we can't. That kind of simplicity lets us divide our components into two categories, and labeling them is much more straightforward than tiring them. Anything that's not critical has the potential to tolerate failures, and so we can start thinking about the failure detection and recovery design of these components.

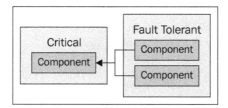

Critical components, versus other components that are tolerant of errors

Detecting and containing errant behavior

Our components should be decoupled from one another, if we're designing an architecture that scales well. Part of that decoupling is errors. Errors that cause one component to fail, should never cause another component to fail. If we can adopt that mantra, everything else becomes simpler. Because if one component fails, we can say with confidence that the failure wasn't caused by another component. From there, it's substantially more straightforward to figure out the cause and deliver a solution.

Decoupling errors in one component from other components is much simpler to do if we have something like an event broker in place. If all inter-component communication is brokered, then that's a good place to implement a mechanism to detect errors and prevent them from propagating to other components. For example, if one component receives an event and runs a callback function that fails, it could have side effects across the entire application, possibly even causing it to fail entirely.

Instead the event broker would detect this error, an exception thrown for example, or an error state code returned by the callback function. In the case of the exception, it doesn't find its way up the **call stack**, because it's caught. The next handlers in the event queue can then receive information about the failed handler—so they can decide what to do, perhaps nothing. What's important is that the error is contained, and its occurrence is communicated to other components.

Following is an example that shows an event broker that's capable of detecting errors and forwarding them on to the next callback for the event:

```
// events.js
// The event broker...
class Events {

    // Trigger an event...
    trigger(name, data) {
        if (name in this.listeners) {
            // We need to know the outcome of the previous handler,
            // so each result is stored here.
            var previous = null;

            return this.listeners[name].map(function(callback) {
                var result;

                // Get the result of running the callback. Notice
                // that it's wrapped in an exception handler. Also
                // notice that callbacks are passed the result
                // of the "previous" callback.
                try {
                    result = previous = callback(Object.assign({
                        name: name
                    }, data), previous);
                } catch(e) {
                    // If the callback raises an exception, the
                    // exception is returned, and also passed to
                    // the next callback. This is how the callbacks
```

```
                    // know if their predecessor failed or not.
                    result = previous = e;
                }

                return result;
            });
        }
    }

}

var events = new Events();

export default events;

// main.js
import events from 'events.js';

// Utility for getting the error message from
// the object. If it's an exception, we can return
// the "message" property. If it has an "error"
// property, we can return that value. Otherwise,
// it's not an error and we return "undefined".
function getError(obj) {
    if (obj instanceof Error) {
        return obj.message;
    } else if (obj && obj.hasOwnProperty('error')) {
        return obj.error;
    }
}

// This callback will be executed first, since it's
// the first to subscribe to the event. It'll randomly
// throw errors.
events.listen('action', (data, previous) => {
    if (Math.round(Math.random())) {
        throw new Error('First callback failed randomly');
    } else {
        console.log('First callback succeeded');
    }
});

// This callback is second in line. It checks if the
```

```
// "previous" result is an error. If so, it will exit
// early by returning the error. Otherwise, it'll randomly
// throw its own error or succeed.
events.listen('action', (data, previous) => {
    var error = getError(previous);
    if (error) {
        console.error(`Second callback failed: ${error}`);
        return previous;
    } else if (Math.round(Math.random())) {
        throw new Error('Second callback failed randomly');
    } else {
        console.log('Second callback succeeded');
    }
});

// The final callback function will check for errors in
// the "previous" result. What's key here is that only
// one of the preceding callbacks will have failed. Because
// the second callback doesn't do anything if the first
// callback fails.
events.listen('action', (data, previous) => {
    var error = getError(previous);
    if (error) {
        console.error(`Third callback failed: ${error}`);
        return previous;
    } else {
        console.log('Third callback succeeded');
    }
});

events.trigger('action');
```

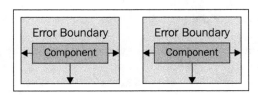

Containing errors means that errors emitted by one component can't affect other components

Disabling defective components

When we fail-fast for the entire application, it's because we're trying to avoid worse problems from materializing. But, what if there's a problem with a component that's completely decoupled from the rest of the components in the system? We can try to recover from the failure, but that's not always possible—if there's a bug, the only recovery option is to patch the code. In the meantime, we could disable the component when recovery isn't an option.

Doing this serves two purposes. First, there's less chance of the errant component spreading its problems around the system. Second, disabling the component, or hiding it completely, prevents any user interaction. This means that there's less chance of the user repeatedly retrying things that eventually lead to other bugs. It shouldn't, because the component is isolated, but still—we don't always know where our design is flawed.

With the problematic component out of the way, we can take some solace in that the user isn't completely out of luck. It's just that there is one aspect of the system that they can't interact with. This gives us a little bit of time to diagnose the issues and patch the problematic component.

The design question is—who is responsible for disabling the component—is it the component itself, or is it the responsibility of some core component that detects the problem? On the one hand, the component turning itself off is a good idea because there may be several steps involved in shutting down safely, so as to keep the rest of the components running smoothly. On the other hand, having something like the event broker shut down problematic components when it encounters them keeps the error handling in one place. The approach we take really depends on the simplest possible solution. If the event broker can safely do this, then that's probably the best bet.

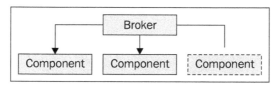

Disabled components don't interact with the rest of the system, which decreases the likelihood of the problematic component causing problems

Gracefully degrading functionality

Disabling components when an error is detected is one thing. It's another thing to handle a failed component and gracefully remove it from the UI. As much as we strive to keep our components loosely coupled with one another, it's a different problem entirely when it comes to the DOM. For example, can we actually remove the DOM elements of a failed component without disrupting the surrounding elements? Or are we better off leaving the elements where they are, but disabling them visually and turning off any JavaScript event handlers?

The approach we take depends on what we're building, that is, the nature of our application. Some applications make it easy to add and remove features, due in part to the composition of our components, but also the general layout of the UI. Avoid thinking that the visual design is just a skin that's detachable from the rest of the application without consequence. In theory, it should be decoupled from the rest of the system, but in practice this notion doesn't scale. If we want to scale, the layout of our elements on the page is relevant, for reasons like failed components, and our ability to disable or remove them without side effects in other places.

We should think of dealing with failed components as shutting them down, because there are usually actions that need to happen—so we can gracefully degrade the user experience. Rarely does the whole feature fail—it's one component, like a router, that causes a feature to be nonfunctional. So, if we turn off the router handlers for a given component, we'll need to turn off other components in order to remove the feature from the UI, and display error messages for the user, and so on. These shutdown semantics need to be considered and tested for any given feature we build. It's not the feature itself we're trying to protect; rather, we're protecting the rest of the system from the feature should it go rogue.

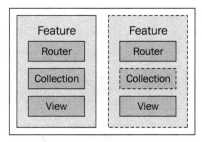

A collection component failed, causing the feature as a whole to go out of service;
but the application as a whole is still functional

Failure recovery

In the preceding section, we started to think about fault tolerance in our frontend code. That is, our application needs to survive the loss of a failed component—at least in the short term. But what if there are certain kinds of errors that we can recover from? So instead of shutting down the component after detecting the error, we would take some alternative course of action; one that would still satisfy the user.

In this section, we'll look at the various ways our components can recover from failed operations. For example, we can retry an operation, or we could flush out the bad state of a component by restarting it. Sometimes, it makes sense to get input from the user on how they wish to proceed during a recovery effort.

Retrying failed operations

If our component executes an operation that fails, it can retry the operation. The operation doesn't even have to be an integral part of the component. But since the component depends on this operation, if it fails, then so does the component. For example, a backend API call can fail, leaving our component that made the call in an uncertain state. API calls are good candidates for retrying in the event of failure.

Whether it's an API call we're retrying, or an operation concerning another component, we have to make sure that it's **idempotent**. This means that *after* the initial operation call, subsequent calls have no side effects. Calling the operation several times in succession will not have a negative impact elsewhere in the system, in other words. Fetch requests—requests that ask the API for data without changing the state of any backend resources—are good candidates for retries. For example, if our fetch request fails because the backend is taking too long, possibly due to competing requests from other users, we could try the request again and get an immediate result. We may not want to continue waiting, but we're safe to retry should we decide to. Next is an example that shows a model that will retry failed fetch attempts:

```
// api.js
// Simulate an API call by returning a promise.
function fetch() {
    return new Promise((resolve, reject) => {

        // After one second, randomly resolve or
        // reject the promise.
        setTimeout(() => {
            if (Math.round(Math.random())) {
                resolve();
```

```
            } else {
                reject();
            }
        }, 1000);

    });
}

export default fetch;

// model.js
import fetch from 'api.js';

// An entity model that's fetched from the API.
export default class Model {

    // Initialized with a "retries" count and an
    // "attempts" counter, used when the requests fail.
    constructor(retries=3) {
        this.attempts = 0;
        this.retries = retries;
    }

    // Returns a new promise where "fetchExecutor()"
    // attempts, and possibly re-attempts to call the API.
    fetch() {
        return new Promise(this.fetchExecutor.bind(this));
    }

    fetchExecutor(resolve, reject) {
        // Call the API and resolve the promise. Also reset the
        // "attempts" counter.
        fetch().then(() => {
            this.attempts = 0;
            resolve();
        }).catch(() => {
            // Make another API request attempt, unless
            // we've already made too many, in which case
            // we can reject the promise.
            if (this.attempts++ < this.retries) {
                console.log('retrying', this.attempts);
                this.fetchExecutor(resolve, reject);
            } else {
```

```
                this.attempts = 0;
                reject(`Max fetch attempts
                    ${this.retries} exceeded`);
            }
        });
    }

};


// main.js
import Model from 'model.js';

var model = new Model();

// Fetch the model, and look at the logging
// output to see how many attempts were made.
model.fetch()
    .then(() => {
        console.log('succeeded');
    })
    .catch((e) => {
        console.error(e);
    });
```

We have to be aware of the types of operations we're performing, and
the types of failures we're receiving. For example, submitting a form
that creates a new resource can fail in a number of ways. If we were
to attempt this operation, and it returned a 503 error, we'd know that
it's safe to retry — because no resources in the back-end were actually
touched. On the other hand, we could get a 500 — meaning that we have
no idea what took place in the backend.

With fetch requests, we don't necessarily need to worry about the type
of failure as much because we're not changing the state of anything. This
means that before retrying an operation, we need to consider the type of
operation, and if it modifies resources, the type of error response.

Restarting components

Components usually have a lifecycle — startup, shutdown, and several phases of existence in between, depending on the type of component. Usually, this lifecycle needs to be kicked-off by whatever creates the component. As the component moves throughout its lifecycle, it changes its internal state. This state could potentially be the source of failures seen later on with the component.

For example, if a component is in a *busy* state, and doesn't process any external requests coming from outside components, then we're likely to see issues elsewhere in the system. Maybe the component is legitimately busy, or maybe something else happened to get it stuck in that state erroneously. If that's that case, then maybe restarting the lifecycle over again would be enough to resolve any issues and get the component in a running state, able to process external requests again.

Essentially, restarting a component is a last-ditch effort to recover from an error. It means that we don't know what's wrong with the component, only that something's not working, and it's wreaking havoc throughout the application. The main complication with restarting components when there's a problem, is that once we've flushed out the bad internal state, the component still needs to pick up where it left off. For instance, if we have a component with a collection that's fetched from the backend, and we restart it, due to problems with the state of the component, then it needs to fetch that collection again.

So before we start designing restart functionality into our components, we need to consider several things. First of all, how do we know when to restart a component? That's generally an application-specific decision to make, but they're mostly centered around edge cases where the component is failing. If there's a bug, then restarting it isn't likely to help, but it also doesn't hurt to try. The other aspect is the restoration of the data source — not the internal state, but the source of the data this application uses. These are two separate things — the internal state is something that's *computed* by the component, and the data is an external source that's *supplied* as input.

We don't want to implement the component restart capability as a mechanism that masks other problems with our code. It's just a good way to think about designing our components. It forces us to think about the various ways the component might get tossed around in the environment. Even just asking the question is worthwhile — what would happen if I restarted this component, or replaced it with a new instance at runtime? We may never actually do these things, and it may not be feasible even if we wanted to. However, going through the exercise means that we'll start designing our components to be more resilient in these scenarios.

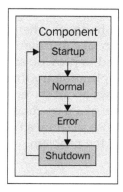

A very high-level view of a component's state cycle

Manual user intervention

If the component that's causing problems is capable of restarting itself, in an effort to rid itself of error states, then we might want to give the user some control over when this happens. For example, if a component generates an error, then we could disable the feature, telling the user that something went wrong with the feature, and ask them if they would like to reload the feature.

The same approach can be taken with retrying failed operations — ask the user if they want to try again. Of course, we have to take the liberty of handling the more mundane retry/restart attempts for the user. When it's obvious that the user wants this action to succeed, and they haven't been waiting too long, then we shouldn't bother them with questions about retrying an operation. That defeats the purpose — which is to be responsive, by giving control back to the user, when our software has encountered a scenario that doesn't allow it to do its job.

We would probably want to declare some sort of threshold that must be met by our restart/retry attempts before seeking input from the user. For instance, the API data we're trying to fetch has timed out twice, and the user is probably growing impatient. So we stop there, and tell the user what's going on — that we're not getting a response from the backend. Should we keep trying, or stop here? Because when our components encounter non-deterministic situations like this, it's better to pass control to a human, who may have a little more insight than our code does.

Our component will happily chug along restarting and retrying things, but only if that's OK with the user. But what happens when the user gives up, they've been through enough torture and want to take affirmative action, rather than letting the wheels spin? Then we probably need to provide some guidance to the user. What else can they do besides let their application try the same thing over and over? Is there anything our component knows about the error, that can be translated for the user? For example, what if the cause of a particular error is fixed by changing a user preference? Then it would make sense to show a friendly, instructive message here, telling them how to go about fixing the problem.

 It's probably best to phrase troubleshooting suggestions as *possible* solutions — not as sure bets. Just in the spirit of avoiding nasty support requests.

When we can't recover from failures...

If we've reached this point in a failure, and the user still isn't getting what they need from our software, there's nothing we can do. As the section title suggests, not everything is recoverable. The backend API isn't always going to be reachable. Our components will have bugs in production environments, sometimes for years before they're even found.

Epic fails like these are akin to our application doing a face plant in front of a crowd of people. Retrying actions just returns the same result. Restarting components have no effect. Asking the user for input isn't going to help, because maybe it's not possible to retry the particular action that's failing, or we just haven't implemented any kind of user input here.

In either case, the solution is to revert to the fail-fast mode of failure — pull the plug on the component, or on the entire application under exceptional circumstances. If we're disabling just the failed component, we have to make sure that our application can function without it. It's back to the plane landing with a single engine analogy — can it be done? If not, then we have to stop the entire application.

All this may sound a little bit drastic at first glance. However, doing so eliminates a whole class of other defects that our support team doesn't have to worry about. There's less chance of new defects being introduced into a live system, due to the side effects of buggy components.

We're playing the odds with scalable error handling, and the odds are in our favor when we don't try to be too clever with our recovery activities.

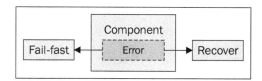

The two failure mode options of a failed component; the choice can be made at runtime, and it isn't necessarily an up-front design decision

Performance and complexity

With robust failure detection and recovery in place, it's time to turn our attention to the performance and complexity implications they introduce. With any large scale JavaScript application, nothing is free — with every gain, there's a new scaling challenge. Failure handling is just one of those gains.

The two closely related scaling factors related to failure handling are performance and complexity. Our software fails in interesting ways, and there's no elegant way to handle them, resulting in complex implementations. Complex code is generally not very good for performance. So we'll start by looking at what makes our exception-handling code slow.

Exception handling

When we handle exceptions in JavaScript, we generally catch all errors that get thrown. Whether it's something we anticipate being thrown, or something that's out of the blue, it's up to the exception handler to then figure out what to do with the error. For example, does it shut the component down, or retry the operation? What's nice about `try`/`catch` statements is that we can ensure that nothing slips through a given section of code uncaught. Because that's when we start seeing side effects across other components.

One way to implement this, as an overarching exception handling mechanism that doesn't let errors through, is in the event broker. Here, we would wrap calls to any event callbacks in a `try`/`catch` block. That way, no matter the outcome of calling an event callback function, the exception handling code can examine the exception and figure out what to do.

Here's the problem though—code that runs within an exception handler pays a performance penalty. JavaScript engines are quite good at optimizing our code just in time. Certain things prevent these optimizations from happening, and exception handlers are one of those things. The problem is magnified when the there're several levels of exception handlers, all the way down the call stack.

How noticeable is this impact, in terms of user-perceptible lag? That depends on the scale of our application—more components means more code running that may not be getting optimized. But in general, this isn't going to be the factor that determines whether our application is slow or not. In conjunction with other determinants, however, it could be important. Having lean exception handling in place at the event broker level is a reasonable trade-off. All our code runs through the try block here, but, we get a lot in return—we can only go fast if we handle failures appropriately.

The nested exception handling, that takes place inside each one of our components, is likely to cause more performance and complexity issues. For example, if our event callback function catches errors, and does a poor job of dealing with them, then we're likely doing more harm than good. It's usually better to let the exceptions be caught in the same place. There are also the performance implications as mentioned previously. We can take a hit at a higher level, but we don't want to take further hits on each one of our components, especially since these will grow in number.

State checking

In addition to exception handling, we have logic that checks the state of our components before executing actions. If the current state is not suitable for the action, then it isn't performed, because doing so could cause problems. This is a kind of proactive exception-handling where we handle any potential error before attempting to do anything, whereas exception handling is more optimistic.

Component states on their own can be simple, but when our code has to check for edge cases, it usually involves checking the state of the component where it lives, but also the state of other components. Not necessarily directly—because our components are decoupled—but indirectly, such as by issuing a query to the main application. This can get quite complicated. And as we add more components, there'll be more state checking to be done there, along with a good chance that our existing state checking code will grow more complex.

Simple state checks are fine if they're coded as an `if` statement, or something along those lines. But what tends to happen is that these edge cases grow as tests fail, and more edge-case-handling gets added to the tangle. If we think about the state of the application as a whole, we'll see that it's just an aggregate sum of all our component states. Given that there are lots of components, each with its own unique states and constraints on what actions can be performed under what circumstances, it's no wonder that we cannot predict how our application will fail. When we start down this path, it's easy to introduce more problems into the system. This is the cost of complexity — where there wasn't a problem before, there is now, thanks to some error handling we added somewhere else.

One approach to ease the complexities of state-checking our components in order to facilitate error handling, is to declaratively bind our operations to conditions that must be satisfied. For example, we could have some kind of mapping with the name of the operation, and a collection of all the conditions to check. Then a generalized mechanism could look at this mapping and figure out whether or not we can execute the action. Using something like this consistently across components will reduce the number of problematic `if` statements.

Notifying other components

Another challenge we face as JavaScript architects is failure handling in a system of decoupled components. We want our components decoupled from one another because it means they're interchangeable, and the system is easier to build and extend. In the context of error handling, this separation acts as a safety net between a failed component and the rest of the system. This is all great news, but we also need to communicate component failures, along with all the other events that take place along the happy path. How do we do this while retaining the loose coupling we have in place?

Let's start by thinking about the event broker — the arbiter of all inter-component communication. If it can deliver all our component events, surely it can deliver error notifications as well? Let's say the broker executes a function callback, and it raises an exception. The exception is caught by the broker, and the details about the error are included as an argument to the next callback function for the event.

Under normal circumstances, the callbacks would receive an error argument, so this would need to be checked for—a minor obstacle with minor overhead. In the case that the function doesn't care what happens before it, then this argument can be safely ignored. Or, if an error is passed, the callback can look at the error and figure out what to do next. If it's this type of error—check the state of this, otherwise, do that, and so on—it may choose to do nothing. The important thing is that the error is communicated, because if we don't want an error in one component to have side effects, then sometimes corrective action needs to be taken in other components, but it needs to know that the error happened.

Logging and debugging

Part of coping with failure in a large-scale JavaScript application is producing the right information. The most obvious place to start is the error console, where uncaught exceptions are logged, or just plain error messages generated using `console.error()`. Some error messages lead to quick fixes, while others send programmers on a wild goose chase.

Apart from logging errors as they happen, we might also want to log situations where something erroneous is about to happen. These are warning messages and they're not used as much as they should be in frontend applications. Warnings are especially useful in diagnosing the more insidious problems with our code, as they leave a trail of clues in the wake of a failure.

The user doesn't necessarily see these logs if they don't have their developer tools window open, and the average user probably doesn't. Instead, we only show them the errors that are relevant to what they're doing in the application. Therefore, we can't just make statements, we have to follow them up with the next steps.

Meaningful error logs

Meaningful error messages go a long way. This is indeed a scaling issue, considering that the effectiveness of the error message directly impacts the developers' ability to resolve issues in a timely manor. Consider error messages that don't contain useful information. When we investigate these failures, much more time is spent piecing together what went wrong. We can use the developer tools in the browser to trace the origin of the error, but that will only get us the location. We'll need better guidance on what went wrong.

Sometimes these ambiguous error messages aren't a big deal, because when we trace their origin in the code, it's immediately obvious what's wrong. Often it's just an edge case that we overlooked, and it's fixed with a few lines of code. Other times, the problem is deeper than that. For example, what if it turns out that the error is actually caused as a side effect of something another component is doing? Does that suggest that we might want to fix the design problem, since we were under the assumption that we didn't have any side effects?

Consider the following error message: `Uncaught TypeError: component.action is not a function`. There's a lot of work in trying to decipher this—unless we're intimately familiar with the code because we interact with it on a daily basis. The problem is that we grow less familiar with our code as our application scales, because there're more components added. This means we spend less time with them, and when they break, it's tough to fix them with a quick turn-around. Unless we have help from the errors themselves. What if the error above were changed to: `ActionError: The "query" component does not support the "save" action`.

Admittedly, having this kind of specific detail in the error messages we generate does add to the complexity of our code. However, the benefits will prove useful if we can strike a balance between providing specific checks and letting our code fail naturally. For example, it's completely pointless to spend time and effort coding an error check and detailed message for something that never happens. Only focus on the scenarios that have a large payoff. Meaning, that if there's a strong likelihood of the error occurring, then that message can point to a quick solution.

When we fail fast, we should throw our own exceptions. This makes the error explicit in the console, and we can provide meaningful information that helps developers diagnose the issue. Throwing exceptions is an easy way to fail fast, because once thrown, the current execution stack stops running.

Warning about potential failures

The difference between an error message and a warning message is that the latter means that the system is still functioning as normal, albeit, not optimally. For example, if we have some quantity constraints in place, like the number of items in a given collection, we could issue a warning when we're nearing that limit. This capability comes with the same concerns as enhanced error messaging—there's more code and complexity involved.

So, what's the point then, if we have strong error handling in place? Warnings are good because they have a visual distinction in the developer tools console where they're displayed. Errors have a dysfunctional connotation, whereas, that's not the point we're making with warnings. We're trying to state that something bad *might* happen. For example, if we were to rev our car engine high, we'd notice that the tachometer needle enters a red zone. This is a warning, meaning that if this behavior continues, something "not good" might happen.

The ambiguity behind warnings is actually helpful, but with errors, we aim for specificity. We want warnings to be generic so that they can be broad assertions about the state of our applications. This means that our logs won't get filled up with little warning messages that start to repeat themselves. At this point they lose all meaning. If they're general, they can aid in the pathology of errors as we diagnose them. They serve as a clue, most of the time, as to what cased the error that happened a few seconds later. If we're troubleshooting with a more savvy user, who might have developer tools open, they can pass these warnings our way. For the less involved users, we need a more friendly approach to troubleshooting.

Informing and instructing users

The errors and warnings we've discussed so far in this section generally end up in the developer tools console. This implies that we're not too concerned whether the user sees it or not. For the messages we want the users to see, they need to be part of the UI – we can't rely on developer tools being open or present at all. Some of the same error message principles apply to the messages we explicitly display to the user. For example, we want to inform the user that something has gone wrong. It's up to us how specific we get with this message. We have to keep the audience in mind here as well – telling them a component state must be such and such before a method can be called, isn't helpful.

However, if we're able to translate the noun of the error into a feature that the user sees and directly interacts with, then it's going to make immediate sense to them. Now they own what's not working. They probably don't care why it's not – what are they going to do with that information? It's better to follow up with instructions. *This is broken, so here's what you need to do.* This is worth the effort to implement because in terms of scale, the software is taking care of a lot of problems we otherwise need human intervention for, which does not scale. It also keeps the users using our software – which is a big scaling influence to begin with.

Sometimes there aren't good instructions. That is, the feature the user needs just isn't working, and there isn't anything they can do about it. However, we can still aim for a message that tells them this feature has stopped working. The error message in the developer tools console probably has a lot more relevant information as to what went wrong. However, we want to avoid raising exceptions without also doing something user-friendly in the UI as well. Then we'll be servicing both audiences—developers and users.

Improving the architecture

We need robust approaches to handle failed components if our architecture is to scale. But that'll only take us so far into the future—because handling the same failures over and over again doesn't scale. Eliminating the possibility of failure, where possible, does scale. Adding new components introduces new failure modes that we need to account for, and we need to offset these by eliminating old failure modes from the equation.

This is done through design; in particular, revised design. The change can be something minor, or it could be a radical shift in direction. It really depends on the frequency, the severity, and the rate of growth. Factor all these together, and we' come up with design trade-offs that enable us to move forward.

There are a number of techniques that can help get us there. For example, when we encounter new failure scenarios, we need a means to consistently document them, we need to better classify our components into critical versus non-critical categories. And as always, we need to keep things simple.

Documenting failure scenarios

End-to-end tests are a great way to document scenarios. In particular, scenarios that cause our software to fail. We can think some of these up, on the fly, as we design and implement our features. But where end-to-end tests shine is in reproducing actual failures that have taken place in a production environment. Not only are these tests essential for reproducing the error so that we know it's fixed, but also for historical preservation.

Over time, we'll accumulate end-to-end tests that model real life scenarios; something one of our customers actually did, resulting in failure. This makes our software stronger, but only at the implementation level. To a degree, our software is defective by design with each end-to-end test we need to account for. The idea is to improve the architecture to a point where some failures simply aren't possible.

Let's say that we have a few end-to-end tests that fail during the fetch of a given collection. It turns out that the way we're sending parameters, with every request, isn't actually needed. Further, the way we're parsing the response can be fixed as well—certain sections are static. These are architectural improvements because they apply generically, across our data model, and they eliminate certain failures because the code that generated the failure is no longer there.

Improving component classification

Critical components cannot fail, they're an integral part of our core application—if they fail, then so does the application. This is why we have so few of them; perhaps a handful of components that touch every component and absolutely need to function as expected. Components that aren't critical, on the other hand, can fail without bringing down the entire application with them. Or, they can attempt to recover from failures, to keep everything running smoothly for the user.

While the classification of our critical components is a relatively static thing, this isn't always the case. For example, we may have a feature component that we thought wasn't critical, and that the application could survive without it. This may have been true in the past, but now our application has grown, and it turns out that this component touches every other component in non-obvious ways—so it's critical that it doesn't fail.

Do critical components ever lose their criticality? It's more likely that they'll be removed from the design entirely than them being downgraded to a non-critical component. However, we need to make sure that we always have a solid understanding of our critical components. This is an important property of our architecture—having components that cannot fail. If they do, then it's considered an entire application failure. We have to keep this architectural property intact as we scale, which often means making sure we recognize new critical components as they're introduced.

Complexity promotes failure

Complex components have lots of internal parts, and they're connected to their environments in many ways. With complexity, we have implicit states, which often aren't discovered till after a component fails. We just can't grasp, mentally, complex design. And when the designers themselves can't grasp the design, they can't possibly grasp all the failure modes.

There're two ways complexity hurts us. The first ways is in triggering failures in the first place. Because of all the moving parts, we miss edge cases that would be obvious in a simpler component. We have to introduce a lot of error handling code to account for the complexity, making the component more complex, and triggering more failures. The cycle repeats itself.

The second way complexity hurts us is in dealing with failures when they do occur. For example, simple components with few moving parts fail in obvious ways. Even the ones we miss and have to go fix later, take no time to repair. This is due to the simple fact that there's so little for us to traverse mentally. Simplicity promotes safety.

Summary

This chapter introduced us to the various failure modes of our large scale JavaScript applications. The fail-fast mode means that once we detect a problem, we stop everything right away, in an effort to prevent further damage. This is often desirable when a critical component of our application fails.

Fault tolerance is an architectural property that means the system is capable of detecting errors, and preventing them from disrupting regular operation. In a JavaScript context, this usually means catching exceptions and preventing them from disrupting other components. There're several ways that a component can recover from an error, including retrying an operation, or restarting itself, to flush out bad states.

Error handling adds to the complexity of our code, and has performance implications if not handled with care. To avoid these, we have to aim for simple components that don't manipulate state, and avoid excessive exception handling. Error messages can help both programmers and users get the information they need to better cope with failures. The ultimate goal is to turn failures into improved design, eliminating the offending code entirely.

JavaScript at scale is indeed achievable, although at times it can seem like an insurmountable obstacle. To get the right answers, we first need to ask the right questions. I hope this book has equipped you with the requisite knowledge to formulate questions around scaling your JavaScript application. Looking at the right scaling influencer, in the right context, at the right time, will provide you with answers.

Index

P

performance and complexity implications
about 225
component state, checking 226
exception handling 225, 226
other components, notifying 227
performance implications
about 138
configurable behavior
performance 138, 141
configurable locale performance 138
configurable theme performance 141
pluggable business logic
about 70
extending, versus configuring 70, 71
stateless business logic 71
preference types
appearance 121-123
behavior 121, 122
locales 121, 122
publish-subscribe model 76

R

referential transparency 155
router configuration
about 113
registration events 114
routes, deactivating 115
static route declarations 114
routers
about 50-54
conflicting 117
events 104, 105
extending 63
initial configuration, logging 119
invalid resource states, handling 120
responsibilities 103, 104
route events, logging 119
troubleshooting 117
working 103
routes
about 51
triggering 112
user action 112
users, redirecting 113

routing approaches
about 101
hash URIs 102
traditional URIs 102, 103

S

scaling constraints
about 183
backend capabilities 192, 193
CPU consumption 190, 191
JavaScript artifact size 184
memory consumption 187
network bandwidth 185, 186
scaling development
about 38
example 41
multiple resources 40
resources hiring, avoiding 46
resources, searching 39-45
responsibilities 39
responsibilities, allocating 45
scaling features
about 30
application value 31
checklist 43
data-driven features 33
example 37
existing features, modifying 34, 35
killer features 32
new services 35
products, competing with 33, 34
real-time data, consuming 36, 37
supporting user groups and roles 35
scaling features checklist
competitor 44
core value proposition 43
coupling, to backend services 45
feasibility, determining 43
features, enhancing 44
frontend, synchronizing with
backend data 45
informed decisions, making 44
user management, integrating into
features 44
scaling influencers
about 2

T

U

V

Thank you for buying
JavaScript at Scale

About Packt Publishing

Packt, pronounced 'packed', published its first book, *Mastering phpMyAdmin for Effective MySQL Management*, in April 2004, and subsequently continued to specialize in publishing highly focused books on specific technologies and solutions.

Our books and publications share the experiences of your fellow IT professionals in adapting and customizing today's systems, applications, and frameworks. Our solution-based books give you the knowledge and power to customize the software and technologies you're using to get the job done. Packt books are more specific and less general than the IT books you have seen in the past. Our unique business model allows us to bring you more focused information, giving you more of what you need to know, and less of what you don't.

Packt is a modern yet unique publishing company that focuses on producing quality, cutting-edge books for communities of developers, administrators, and newbies alike. For more information, please visit our website at www.packtpub.com.

About Packt Open Source

In 2010, Packt launched two new brands, Packt Open Source and Packt Enterprise, in order to continue its focus on specialization. This book is part of the Packt Open Source brand, home to books published on software built around open source licenses, and offering information to anybody from advanced developers to budding web designers. The Open Source brand also runs Packt's Open Source Royalty Scheme, by which Packt gives a royalty to each open source project about whose software a book is sold.

Writing for Packt

We welcome all inquiries from people who are interested in authoring. Book proposals should be sent to author@packtpub.com. If your book idea is still at an early stage and you would like to discuss it first before writing a formal book proposal, then please contact us; one of our commissioning editors will get in touch with you.

We're not just looking for published authors; if you have strong technical skills but no writing experience, our experienced editors can help you develop a writing career, or simply get some additional reward for your expertise.

JavaScript and JSON Essentials

ISBN: 978-1-78328-603-4   Paperback: 120 pages

Successfully build advanced JSON-fueled web applications with this practical, hands-on guide

1. Deploy JSON across various domains.

2. Facilitate metadata storage with JSON.

3. Build a practical data-driven web application with JSON.

Learning JavaScript Data Structures and Algorithms

ISBN: 978-1-78355-487-4   Paperback: 218 pages

Understand and implement classic data structures and algorithms using JavaScript

1. Learn how to use the most used data structures such as array, stack, list, tree, and graphs with real-world examples.

2. Get a grasp on which one is best between searching and sorting algorithms and learn how to implement them.

3. Follow through solutions for notable programming problems with step-by-step explanations.

Please check **www.PacktPub.com** for information on our titles

Object-Oriented JavaScript

ISBN: 978-1-84719-414-5   Paperback: 356 pages

Create scalable, reusable high-quality JavaScript applications, and libraries

1. Learn to think in JavaScript, the language of the web browser.

2. Object-oriented programming made accessible and understandable to web developers.

3. Do it yourself: experiment with examples that can be used in your own scripts.

4. Write better, more maintainable JavaScript code.

Functional Programming in JavaScript

ISBN: 978-1-78439-822-4   Paperback: 172 pages

Unlock the powers of functional programming hidden within JavaScript to build smarter, cleaner, and more reliable web apps

1. Discover what functional programming is, why it's effective, and how it's used in JavaScript.

2. Understand and optimize JavaScript's hidden potential as a true functional language.

3. Explore the best coding practices for real-world applications.

Please check **www.PacktPub.com** for information on our titles

www.ingramcontent.com/pod-product-compliance
Lightning Source LLC
Chambersburg PA
CBHW060534060326
40690CB00017B/3482